Christ in the Gospels
of the Ordinary Sundays

Raymond E. Brown, S.S.

Christ in the Gospels of the Ordinary Sundays

Essays on the Gospel Readings
of the Ordinary Sundays
in the Three-Year Liturgical Cycle

A Liturgical Press Book

The Liturgical Press
Collegeville, Minnesota

Cover design by Mary Jo Pauly

Nihil obstat: Robert C. Harren, *Censor deputatus.*
Imprimatur: ✠ John F. Kinney, Bishop of St. Cloud, June 15, 1998.

1	2	3	4	5	6	7	8

Library of Congress Cataloging-in-Publication Data

Brown, Raymond Edward.
    Christ in the Gospels of the ordinary Sundays : essays on the Gospel readings of the ordinary Sundays in the three-year liturgical cycle / Raymond E. Brown.
        p.   cm.
    Includes bibliographical references.
    ISBN 0-8146-2542-8 (alk. paper)
    1. Bible. N.T. Gospels—Criticism, interpretation, etc.
I. Title.
BS2555.2.B73   1998
226'.06—dc21   98-25613
                                                                                      CIP

Foreword

Previously in five books of format comparable to this book (see list on the last printed page of this volume), The Liturgical Press has published my reflections on the liturgical New Testament readings for Advent, Christmas, Holy Week, Easter, and the season leading up to Pentecost—in short, the Scripture used in that half of the liturgical year where special periods are devoted to salvation history from the coming of Jesus Christ to the coming of the Holy Spirit. In this book I plan to discuss the Gospels as they are used in the other half of the liturgical year, designated (not too imaginatively) as "the Ordinary Time." Many liturgists look on this as the time of the church when we turn from reflecting on the mystery of Christ in itself to considering directly how that mystery affects the lives of those who believe in him.

Here in a triennial cycle, the Lectionary of the A Year takes its consecutive readings from Matthew, the B Year from Mark, and the C Year from Luke. Passages from John are read every year during the last part of Lent and the postEaster season till Pentecost. (Actually the arrangement is more complicated, and so at the end of the book I shall supply a table illustrating in more detail the use of the Gospels in the Sunday and seasonal Lectionary.) The first chapter below will discuss how a Gospel was formed because I am firmly convinced that, although we read and hear a Gospel passage every Sunday, most people have only the vaguest idea what a Gospel is. Then a chapter each will be devoted to the four Gospels. Clergy frequently ask about homily guides for each Sunday. That is *not* what I intend to supply here, for The Liturgical Press already offers a volume of such guides written by Reginald Fuller. Rather, I want to give an overall picture of each Gospel: how it shapes its narrative, its theological emphases, and what it is trying to say to readers/hearers—a larger picture that supplies a context for understanding the individual readings. I believe strongly that every time we start the Ordinary Sundays of a new year (and every Lent or postEaster season in the case of John) preachers need to familiarize themselves with the type of material presented in these chapters *and to share such material with their Sunday audiences* so that all grasp how unique is the Gospel, the pages of which are now being opened in church. Obviously the same thing may be said for Bible study groups who are beginning to reflect on the Gospel of the year.

In the half century in which I have had the good fortune to be immersed in the study of the Bible, especially the New Testament, a particular grace accorded me was the teaching and example of scholars who loved church liturgy. To mention only two, William O'Shea, S.S., when I was in the seminary, and Myles M. Bourke, who was pastor at Corpus Christi Church when I was teaching at Union Theological Seminary, New York. They enabled me to appreciate how the liturgy well conducted and the readings well proclaimed constitute the most homogeneous context for understanding why Gospels were written and what they were intended to accomplish. With gratitude to all those who have contributed to that insight I dedicate this volume.

Contents

Abbreviations

JBap	John the Baptist
Matt	Matthew (Gospel)
NT	New Testament
OT	Old Testament

Chapter 1

Understanding How Gospels Were Written and Their Use in the Sunday Liturgy

Many people probably think of the Gospels as biographies of Jesus. In any modern sense they are not. Some of the most basic biographical information about Jesus (when and where born, name of one parent) is absent from Mark and from John. Even more people would be unaware of how much one Gospel differs from another. The sharp differences not only raise further difficulties for the biographical approach (and perhaps create fears about the historical truth of the Gospels) but also lead into the question of the origin and goal of the Gospels.

CHURCH TEACHING ON THE THREE STAGES OF GOSPEL FORMATION

Fortunately the Church has given us a very helpful guide for dealing with these issues—a guide that wins the approval of most centrist scholars. I refer to the Instruction on the Historical Truth of the Gospels issued by the Roman Pontifical Biblical Commission in 1964 (the substance of which was incorporated into Vatican II's Dogmatic Constitution on Divine Revelation in 1965).

When some Catholics are told that the Gospels are not necessarily literal accounts of the ministry of Jesus, they become suspicious of the "orthodoxy" of the person who makes such a claim. It may be important, therefore, to stress that this Instruction, which offers that evaluation, constitutes binding teaching of the Catholic Church on all its members. Let me use the Instruction as a springboard to explain the Gospels by elaborating on its implications.[1] No better guidance can be offered in

---

[1] An English translation of the actual text appears in the Appendix to my small book *Reading the Gospels with the Church* (Cincinnati: St. Anthony Messenger

preaching about the Gospels at the beginning of each liturgical year, in Bible discussion groups, and in catechetical teaching.

The Instruction orients its treatment of the reliability of the Gospels by insisting that diligent attention should be paid to THE THREE STAGES OF TRADITION by which the life and teaching of Jesus have come down to us. Those three stages, which follow chronologically one upon the other, are the Ministry of Jesus, the Preaching of the Apostles, and the Writing by the Evangelists. We would not be far from common scholarly opinion if we assigned one-third of the 1st century AD to each, since Jesus died *ca.* 30–33, the main preaching apostles were dead by the mid-60s, and the evangelists probably wrote in the period 65–100.

STAGE ONE: THE PUBLIC MINISTRY OR ACTIVITY OF JESUS OF NAZARETH

We may date this to the first third of the 1st century AD. The Instruction does not concern itself with Jesus' birth and infancy.[2] Rather, it focuses on the words and deeds of Jesus from the time of his calling the first disciples. Jesus did noteworthy things (which the first three Gospels label "deeds of power" and we refer to as miracles) as he orally proclaimed his message. At the same time, he chose companions who traveled with him and saw and heard what he said and did. Their memories of his words and deeds supplied the raw Jesus material or Jesus tradition that would be preached in Stage Two (below). These memories were already selective, since they concentrated on what pertained to Jesus' proclamation of God, not the many details of ordinary existence, some of which would have been included if a biography were intended.

Press, 1996). With the kind agreement of that press, I am adapting material from Chapter 2 of that book for the present chapter.

[2] Several years after the Instruction was issued, the Roman Pontifical Commission did meet to discuss the historicity of the infancy narratives, presumably with the hope of issuing a similar instruction pertinent to them—a project never completed. I have treated these narratives in my companion Liturgical Press books *A Coming Christ in Advent* and *An Adult Christ at Christmas*.

Christ in the Gospels of the Ordinary Sundays

On a practical level it is important for modern readers to keep reminding themselves that these were memories of what was said and done by a Jew who lived in Galilee, Jerusalem, and environs in the 20s.[3] Jesus' manner of speaking, the problems he faced, his vocabulary and outlook, were those of that specific time, place, and circumstance. Often he had new ways of looking at things, but his newness did not remove him from his time and place. Many failures to understand Jesus and misapplications of his thought stem from the fact that people who read the Gospels remove him from space and time and imagine that Jesus was dealing with issues he never encountered.

Both liberal and conservative Christians make that mistake. For instance, liberal pacifist Christians may ask whether Jesus would serve as a soldier in a modern war (in Vietnam or in the Gulf). The exact, even if somewhat brutal, answer to such a question is that a Galilean Jew would not have known of the existence of Vietnam or of mechanized war. A better-phrased question would be: In fidelity to what Jesus taught and to his example, what is a *Christian's* duty in relation to a modern war? Conservative Christians often want to settle questions of church structure and practice by appealing to Jesus. Once after a series of lectures on the origin of the church a well-intentioned member of the audience asked me: "Why didn't Jesus prevent all future confusion by saying, 'I came to found the Roman Catholic Church, the Bishop of Rome or the Pope will be the leader of the Church, and everyone must obey him'?" The difficulty is that Jesus is recorded only twice in all the Gospels as having spoken of "church" (Matt 16:18; 18:17, in the second of which he is clearly talking about a local community). Thus there is little recorded proof that he spent much time thinking about the structure of a future church. Rather, he was concerned with proclaiming God's kingdom or rule to those whom he encountered

---

[3] Such a reference to Jesus will often raise the immediate objection "Was he not Son of God?" One must remember, however, that Christian dogma describes him equally as true God and *true man*.

Chapter 1. Understanding Gospels

in his lifetime. Moreover, a Galilean Jew would scarcely have thought of an institution in Rome where the emperor was, or of categories like "pope" and "bishop." A better phrasing of the issue is whether the community called "church" that emerged from the preaching of his followers, and the centralizing of that church in Rome where Peter died as a martyr, are valid developments from what he proclaimed, and in that sense may be said to be founded by him. Catholics answer yes, for they trace *a line of development* from what Jesus said and did to what the apostles said and did, and to later growth. In Christian faith the Jesus tradition truly has decisive ramifications for problems and issues that did not appear in his lifetime, but *the Holy Spirit* clarifies these ramifications by helping to translate from Jesus' time to subsequent periods.

Church life and teaching are the usual context of such translation. That is why, when we meet together to worship on Sunday, the Gospels are not simply read but also preached on so as to bring out their implications for our time. When Church documents speak about the actions of "Christ" or "Jesus Christ," they are not simply talking about the Jesus as he was in his public ministry but about the Jesus portrayed in apostolic preaching and reflected on in subsequent tradition and development.

STAGE TWO: THE (APOSTOLIC) PREACHING ABOUT JESUS
We may date this to the second third of the 1st century AD. The Biblical Commission Instruction contains this clause: "After Jesus rose from the dead and his divinity was clearly perceived." This is a recognition by the Catholic Church that during the ministry of Jesus, although his disciples followed him they did not fully perceive who he was. Thus in this stage a whole new perception colors the Jesus tradition.

Those who had seen and heard Jesus during his public ministry had their following of him confirmed through appearances of the risen Jesus (1 Corinthians 15:5-7) and came to full faith in him as the one through whom God had brought salvation to Israel and eventually the whole world. They vocalized this faith

Christ in the Gospels of the Ordinary Sundays

through the titles under which we find Jesus confessed (Messiah/Christ, Lord, Savior, Son of God, etc.), all of which were gradually transformed by the perception of his divinity. Such postresurrectional faith illumined the memories of what the disciples had seen and heard during the preresurrectional period, and so they proclaimed his words and deeds with enriched significance. This was not a distortion of the Jesus tradition from Stage One; rather it involved a perception of what was already there but had not previously been recognized. (Modern readers, accustomed to a media goal of uninvolved, factual reporting, need to understand that this was not at all the atmosphere of early Christian preaching, which was committed and interpretative.)

We speak of these preachers as "apostolic" because they understood themselves as sent forth (Greek: *apostellein*) by the risen Jesus; their preaching is often described as kerygmatic proclamation *(kērygma)* intended to bring others to faith. Eventually the circle of missionary preachers was enlarged beyond the original companions of Jesus, and the faith experiences of all the preachers enriched what they had received and were now proclaiming.

Another factor operative in this stage of development was the necessary adaptation of the preaching to a new audience. If Jesus was a Galilean Jew of the first third of the 1st century, by mid-century the Gospel was being preached in cities to urban Jews and Gentiles in Greek, a language that Jesus did not normally speak (if he spoke it at all or knew more than a few phrases). This change of language involved translation in the broadest sense of that term, that is, a rephrasing of the message in vocabulary and patterns ("literary forms," in the terminology of the Instruction) that would make it intelligible and alive for new audiences.

In terms of vocabulary, sometimes the rephrasing affected incidentals, for instance, Luke 5:19 substitutes a tile roof familiar to a Greek audience for the Palestinian village-style roof of pressed clay and branches through which a hole was opened, as

Chapter 1. Understanding Gospels

envisioned in Mark 2:4. But other choices had theological repercussions. For instance, Jesus spoke in Aramaic at the Last Supper of his "flesh and blood." While the more literal Greek translation, *sarx*, "flesh," is attested in John 6:51, the first three Gospels and 1 Corinthians 11:24 chose an idiomatic Greek translation, *sōma*, "body," for the eucharistic component. That choice may have facilitated the figurative use of "body" in the theology of the body of Christ of which Christians are members (1 Corinthians 12:12-27). Thus developments in this preaching period of the Jesus tradition served the growth of Christian theology.

Another type of development came from encountering new issues that Jesus never dealt with. The first three Gospels and Paul agree that Jesus took a severe stance against divorce and remarriage: If a man divorces his wife and marries another, he commits adultery. But Jesus was dealing with Jews—how was his demand to be applied once Christianity began to be preached among Gentiles? Jewish women could not divorce Jewish men, but in many Gentile areas women *could* divorce men. Mark 10:12 (and Mark alone) has a second demand: If a woman divorces her husband and marries another, she commits adultery. Jesus probably never said that, but it was the obvious corollary of his teaching as the preachers encountered this new possibility. Similarly Matt 5:32; 19:9 (and Matt alone) adds an exceptive phrase: If a man divorces his wife, except for *porneia*, and marries another, he commits adultery. On the basis of other NT uses (1 Corinthians 5:1; Acts 15:20) it seems likely that by *porneia* Matthew means unions within the forbidden degrees of kindred—"forbidden" and deemed impure by the Mosaic Law and therefore not encountered among Jews but encountered among Gentiles by the preachers. Matthew is teaching that a man not only can but should divorce a wife who is close kinfolk because that is no marriage at all.

We may find it odd that such expansions (or "explications," to use the language of the Instruction) are included *within* the words of Jesus. If we were writing the account, we would have

Christ in the Gospels of the Ordinary Sundays

Jesus' words in the body of the text and add explanatory footnotes in order to apply his teaching to situations unforeseen by him. But one cannot preach with footnotes, and both original word and explication became part of the preached Jesus tradition.[4]

I hope these examples help to show how remarkably formative was this Stage Two of Gospel development. While staying substantially faithful to "what was really said and done by Jesus" and in that sense remaining historical, it moved away from exact literal retention and reproduction and thus kept the Jesus tradition alive, meaningful, and salvific, even as it was in Stage One when it originated.

STAGE THREE: THE WRITTEN GOSPELS

We may date this to the last third of the 1st century AD. Although in the middle of the previous period as the Jesus tradition was being preached, some early written collections (now lost) would have appeared, and although preaching based on *oral* preservation and development of the Jesus tradition continued well into the 2d century, the era from 65 to 100 was probably when all four canonical Gospels were written.

According to titles ("The Gospel according to . . .") attached in the middle or late 2d century, two Gospels were attributed to the eyewitness apostles Matthew and John and two to "apostolic men" who themselves were not eyewitnesses, Mark, the companion of Peter, and Luke, the companion of Paul. Relatively few modern scholars, however, think that any evangelist

---

[4] Paul, when writing letters, could be more precise. In 1 Corinthians 7:10-11 he presents as a word of the Lord that a man should not divorce his wife and that any woman separated from her husband cannot remarry. But then a few verses later (7:12-15) by a word of his own he deals with a situation that Jesus never dealt with—a word that he stresses is *not* a word of the Lord. In the case of a believing Christian married to a non-believer, if they cannot live together in peace and the unbelieving partner desires to separate, let it be so. If Paul were writing a Gospel, such an exception might very well have found its way into the text describing Jesus' attitude toward marriage!

Chapter 1. Understanding Gospels

was an eyewitness of the ministry of Jesus. This surely represents a change of view. Yet the shift may not be so sharp as first seems, for the early traditions about authorship may not always have been referring to the writer in our sense of the one who put the Gospel on papyrus. Ancient attribution may have been more concerned with the one responsible for the tradition enshrined in a particular Gospel, the *author*ity behind the Gospel, or the one who wrote one of the main sources of the Gospel. The section of the Instruction of the Biblical Commission that treats Stage Three does not deal with this question directly but takes care to speak of "apostles" in Stage Two and of "sacred authors/writers" in Stage Three, allowing the interpretation that two different sets of people were involved.[5]

The wide recognition that the evangelists were *not* eyewitnesses of Jesus' ministry is important for understanding the differences among the Gospels. In the older approach wherein eyewitness testimony was directly posited, it was very difficult to explain differences among the Gospels. How could eyewitness John report the cleansing of the Temple at the beginning of the ministry in his chapter 2 and eyewitness Matthew report the cleansing of the Temple at the end of the ministry in his chapter 21? To reconcile them it was maintained that the cleansing of the Temple happened twice and that each evangelist chose to report only one of the two instances. Many other examples of improbable reconciliations stemming from the theory of direct eyewitness accuracy can be offered. Since Matt has a Sermon on the Mount and Luke has a similar Sermon on the Plain (Matt 5:1; Luke 6:17), there must have been a plain on the side of the mountain! Since Matt has the Lord's Prayer taught in that sermon and Luke has it later on the road to Jerusalem (Matt 6:9-13;

---

[5] Although in the early 1900s the Pontifical Biblical Commission taught that substantially the apostle Matthew stood behind Matt and the apostle John wrote John, "full freedom" about those decrees was acknowledged in 1956 by the Secretary of the Commission. As a result there are no longer binding Catholic Church positions about the date or authorship of the Gospels but only on issues where the decrees affected faith and morals.

Christ in the Gospels of the Ordinary Sundays

Luke 11:2-4), the disciples must have forgotten it, so that Jesus repeated it! Mark 10:46 places the healing of the blind man after Jesus left Jericho; Luke 18:35; 19:1 places it before Jesus entered Jericho; perhaps Jesus was leaving the site of OT Jericho and entering the site of NT Jericho!

On the other hand, if direct eyewitness writing was not involved, these harmonizing improbabilities can be avoided. Each evangelist was the recipient of preached Jesus tradition, but there was little in those reports of what Jesus said and did that would clarify the respective where and when. Yet the evangelists, who themselves were not eyewitnesses, had a task that the preachers of Stage Two never had, namely, to shape a sequential narrative from Jesus' baptism to his resurrection. If we suppose that the first and fourth evangelists had received a form of the story of the cleansing of the Temple from an intermediate source, and neither evangelist knew when it occurred during the public ministry, then each placed it where it seemed best in the sequence he was fashioning.

This leads to the insight that the Gospels have been arranged in *logical* order, not necessarily in *chronological* order. Each evangelist has ordered the material according to his understanding of Jesus and his desire to portray Jesus in a way that would meet the spiritual needs of the community to which he was addressing the Gospel. Thus the evangelists emerge as full authors of the Gospels, shaping, developing, and pruning the transmitted Jesus tradition, and as full theologians, orienting that tradition to a particular goal. The Biblical Commission Instruction teaches, "From the many things handed down, they selected some things, reduced others to a synthesis, (still) others they explicated as they kept in mind the situation of the churches."

This means that Stage Three of Gospel formation moved the end-product Gospels still another step further from being literal records of the ministry of Jesus (Stage One). Not only did decades of developing and adapting the Jesus tradition through preaching intervene in Stage Two, but the evangelists themselves reshaped what they received.

Chapter 1. Understanding Gospels

We are children of our time, and so we are curious about Stage One. However, judgments about details of Jesus' life in the first third of the 1st century require painstaking scholarship; and when properly phrased, those judgments use the language of "possibly" or "probably"—rarely "certainly." Indeed, a wise caution is to be extremely skeptical when you read that some scholars are claiming that now they know exactly how much (or how little!) is literally historical in the Gospels—most of the time they are proposing what they want to be historical to fit their own theology.

How can today's preachers, then, know what to preach, and today's hearers know what to believe? It is ridiculous to maintain that Christian proclamation and faith should be changed by every new vagary of scholarship. Rather, preaching and reception are to be based on Stage Three, not on uncertain theories about Stage One. In the wisdom of God we were not given eyewitness notes from Stage One but written Gospels from Stage Three, and those Gospels actually exist, while scholarly reconstructions remain theoretical. *The Gospels are what was inspired by the Holy Spirit,* and Christians believe that the Holy Spirit guided the process of Gospel formation, guaranteeing that the end-product Gospels reflect the truth that God sent Jesus to proclaim.

Stage Three, if properly understood, also has consequences for more conservative Christians. In the history of biblical interpretation much time has been spent in harmonizing Gospel differences, not only in minor matters but also on a large scale. For instance, "Lives of Christ" try to make one sequential narrative out of the very different Matthean and Lucan infancy narratives, or out of Luke's account of appearances of the risen Jesus in Jerusalem and Matthew's account of an appearance on a mountain in Galilee. Besides asking whether this is possible, we need to ask whether such harmonization is not a distortion. In an outlook of faith, divine providence gave us four different Gospels, not a harmonized version; and it is to the individual Gospels, each with its own viewpoint, that we should look. Harmonization, instead of enriching, impoverishes.

Christ in the Gospels of the Ordinary Sundays

The "bottom line" of this discussion based on the Roman Instruction is that modern scholarship creates no embarrassment about the Church's traditional insistence that the Gospels are historical accounts of the ministry of Jesus, provided that, as the Church also insists, "historical" not be understood in any crassly literal sense. Indeed, a 1993 Pontifical Biblical Commission statement about different methods of interpretation is harsher than the 1964 Instruction in criticizing undue stress on historical inerrancy and the historicizing of material that was not historical from the start.

To some Christians any thesis that does not present the Gospels as literal history implies that they are not true accounts of Jesus. Truth, however, must be evaluated in terms of the intended purpose. The Gospels might be judged untrue if the goal was strict reporting or exact biography. If the goal, however, was to bring readers/hearers to a faith in Jesus that leads them to accept God's rule or kingdom, then adaptations that made the Gospels less than literal by adding the dimension of faith and by adjusting to new audiences facilitated that goal and thus enhanced the truth of the Gospels. The Instruction is lucidly clear: "The doctrine and life of Jesus were not simply reported for the sole purpose of being remembered, but were 'preached' so as to offer the church a basis of faith and morals."

THE USE OF THE GOSPELS IN THE LITURGY

How does this discussion affect the liturgical use of the Gospels? In particular I am concerned with how each Gospel is used in the Sunday liturgy, the context in which the doctrine and life of Jesus are most often preached. Clearly an understanding of Stage Three inculcates respect for the individuality of each Gospel, and accordingly in the last half of the 20th century the Roman Catholic Church felt the need to replace the one-year Lectionary that paid no attention to Gospel individuality. In it, without any discernible theological pattern, the reading was taken one Sunday from Matt, another Sunday from Luke; and Mark was practically never used (on the thesis that

Chapter 1. Understanding Gospels

everything in Mark was found in Matt or Luke). A liturgical re-formation introduced a triennial Sunday Lectionary, where in the first or A Year the Gospel readings are primarily taken from Matt, in the second or B Year from Mark, and in the third or C Year from Luke.[6] This change of Lectionary recognizes that se-lections should be read sequentially from the same Gospel if one is to do justice to the theological orientation given to those passages by the individual evangelist. For example, a parable that appears in all three Synoptic Gospels can have different meanings depending on the sequence in which each evangelist has placed it. Other Churches have followed the Catholic lead in setting up a triennial Lectionary, producing the admirable situation that Christians of diverse background are hearing the same Scripture on Sundays—an important ecumenical step to-ward unity!

* * *

In this book I want to supply assistance in appreciating the Gospels in the three-year Sunday Lectionary. In principle the usage is simple, but there are some complications. As I ex-plained above in the Foreword, I shall be concerned with the readings on the Ordinary Sundays of the year, not the festal pe-riods of Advent, Christmas, Holy Week, and Easter through to Pentecost, on which I have already written books in this Liturgi-cal Press series (see the final printed page of this volume).

How are the Gospels used on the Ordinary Sundays of the year? This question concerns Matt, Mark, and Luke—the three Synop-tic Gospels. (Actually, I shall devote a chapter to the usage of John in the days after Christmas and in Lent, since I have not treated that previously.) For practical purposes one must think of beginning the sequential reading of the three Synoptic Gospels with **the Third Sunday of the Ordinary Time.** In each

[6] In this book I am chiefly concerned with Sunday Gospel readings, but the distinctiveness of the individual Gospels is also acknowledged in the weekday Lectionary, where (with allowance for festal exceptions) in the course of each year the three Gospels are read sequentially in the order Mark, Matt, Luke.

Christ in the Gospels of the Ordinary Sundays

of the three Gospels this means starting consecutive Lectionary readings with Jesus' activities after JBap has been removed from public activity because he has been arrested by Herod **(starting respectively with Matt 4:12-23 in Year A; Mark 1:14-20 in Year B; Luke 4:14-21 in Year C[7]).**

Now no Gospel as it stands in the NT begins there, so why this lack of synchronization between NT and liturgy? Let me devote a paragraph to the complicated answer, which lies in the awkwardness of combining festal and ordinary times in the liturgy. In the NT Matt and Luke begin with two chapters of infancy narrative; they are read in late Advent, Christmastime, and Epiphany. There follows in the NT the account of the public ministry of JBap (Matt 3:1-12; Luke 3:1-6, which coincide with the opening of Mark [1:1-8]). The liturgy reads that account on the 2d Sunday of Advent as part of its thesis that JBap is a key figure in the preparation for the coming of Christ, to be celebrated on Christmas. Then in the NT the three Synoptic Gospels recount the story of the baptism of Jesus; and the liturgy reads this on the feast of the Baptism (Matt 3:13-17 in Year A; Mark 1:7-11 in Year B; Luke 3:15-16,21-22 in Year C), always celebrated on the Sunday following the Epiphany and thus replacing the First Sunday of the Ordinary Time. (The Second Sunday of the Ordinary Time respects an old liturgical theme of different epiphanies or manifestations of Jesus.[8]) In the NT the Synoptic Gospels[9] next recount the temptation or testing of Jesus after forty days in the desert (Matt 4:1-11; Mark 1:12-13; Luke 4:1-13), but the Lectionary again cedes to an ancient tradition by

[7] Actually on that Sunday the Lectionary begins with the Lucan Prologue, 1:1-4, and then follows immediately with 4:14. I shall comment on this in Chapter Four, below.

[8] Revealed by a star to the Magi (Epiphany proper, often celebrated on Sunday), by a heavenly voice at the baptism (feast of the Baptism), and by Jesus at Cana, who changes water to the best wine (described only in John 2:1-12). Now on the Second Sunday John 1:29-34 is read in Year A; 1:35-42 in B; 2:1-12 in C.

[9] Luke is an exception, for it follows the baptism with a genealogy of Jesus (3:23-38) and only then narrates the temptation. This genealogy is never used in the Lectionary.

Chapter 1. Understanding Gospels

reading the Gospel accounts of the temptation on the First Sunday of Lent, respectively in Years A, B, and C.[10] All this is why only on the Third Sunday of the Ordinary Time the sequential readings of the Synoptic Gospels begin respectively with Matt 4:12; Mark 1:14; and Luke 4:14. (That sequential reading continues until the First Sunday of Lent and then picks up again after Pentecost.[11])

Important Note: I wish to alert *all* who use the Sunday Gospel Lectionary—although those whose task is to preach on it may need especially to be put on their guard. It is odd to begin a year's sequential reading of Matt, or Mark, or Luke on the *3d* Sunday of the year, especially when one's sense of liturgy has been shaped by the preceding Advent, Christmas, Epiphany, Baptism feasts, and the immediately preceding passage from John.[12] One's tendency is simply to concentrate on the Gospel narrative of the 3d Sunday with Jesus at Capernaum, or the Sea of Galilee, or Nazareth, and to proceed without any attention to the fact that this narrative is the entree into a great Gospel that will be one's companion for the rest of the year, and without asking who is this Jesus of whom we hear in the Gospel. In other words, to begin without reflecting on what has gone before and what is going to follow. Rather, on this 3d Sunday preachers should proclaim with enthusiasm: "Today we begin to read seriously the Gospel according to Matthew, or Mark, or Luke—one of the four fundamental portrayals of Jesus

---

[10] Similarly, sequence is broken by the custom of assigning accounts of the transfiguration in the Synoptic Gospels to the 2d Sunday of Lent in Years A, B, and C respectively.

[11] The number of Sundays of the Ordinary Time before Lent run from five to nine, depending on when Easter occurs. Although we speak of the resumption of Ordinary Sundays after Pentecost, the celebration of Trinity Sunday and (in many places) of Corpus Christi on Sunday delays that resumption for one or two weeks. The number of Ordinary Sundays in the total year varies—the 34th (Christ the King) always being used as the last.

[12] It is even harder to have a sense of beginning John when one starts sequential readings from that Gospel in the middle of Lent. But I shall leave that problem till Chapter Five, below.

Christ in the Gospels of the Ordinary Sundays

Christ on which the church bases its understanding of what God's Son was like when he walked on the face of this earth, of the values he would have us live by, and of how he accomplished our salvation."

And to underline that, those whose task is to proclaim the Gospel might ask themselves and the Sunday congregation three basic questions. *First*, do we really understand what we are saying or hearing when we speak Sunday after Sunday of a reading from "the 'Gospel' according to . . ."? Do we understand what a Gospel is and why it was written? It is to answer that question that I have placed this Chapter first in the book. *Second*, do we have any idea what Matthew's Gospel is, or Mark's, or Luke's, why it is distinctive and what it is trying to say? *Third*, how does this Sunday passage lead us into the Gospel, and fit its purpose? With adaptation that third question will need to be asked every Ordinary Sunday all year long as a reminder of the answer to the first and second questions. It is to help with the second and third questions that I have written below a Chapter on each Gospel.

Chapter 1. Understanding Gospels

Chapter 2

The Gospel according to Matthew[13]
(Liturgical Year A)

Although modern scholars generally begin their Gospel studies with Mark, the oldest of the written Gospels, Matt stood first in most ancient biblical witnesses and has been the church's Gospel par excellence. Indeed, Matt has served as the foundational document of the church, rooting it in the teaching of Jesus—a church built on rock against which the gates of hell would not prevail (only Matt 16:18). Matt's Sermon on the Mount, the (eight) Beatitudes, and the Lord's Prayer are among the most widely known treasures in the Christian heritage. (It is always awesome to stop and think how impoverished we would be without the contributions peculiar to each Gospel.) Organizational skill and clarity, plus a penchant for unforgettable images, have given this Gospel priority as the church's teaching instrument. Consequently it is no surprise that in the triennial Lectionary the church reads Matt on the Sundays of the first or A Year.

INTRODUCTORY OBSERVATIONS

I have contended above that on the *3d Sunday of the Ordinary Time,* when for all practical purposes we begin reading the Gospel of the liturgical year, besides reflecting on what a Gospel is one should appreciate in a general way what makes the particular Gospel distinctive. Accordingly, at the beginning of each Chapter I shall give a summary of information about the Gospel

[13] A minor point: Lectors in church should be trained to read exactly the title that the Lectionary gives to the reading (not "*of* Matthew" or "according to *St.* Matthew" or, worst of all, the cutesy rendering, "The Good News St. Matthew wrote to us"—no NT book was written to us, even though all have meaning for us.). These Lectionary Gospel titles are the oldest we know, and we should respect them.

Christ in the Gospels of the Ordinary Sundays

and an outline of the whole,[14] that is, background details meant to enrich the readers' and hearers' understanding.

Matt was probably written in the period AD 80–90 in the vicinity of Antioch in Syria, a major city with a sizable Jewish population. From Jerusalem, Jewish missionaries came to Antioch proclaiming Christ in the 30s, and they made converts not only among fellow Jews but also among Gentiles. Barnabas and Paul were important figures in the Antioch Christian community by the early 40s (Acts 13:1-3). In the late 40s the mixed Christian community at Antioch was a factor in provoking the opposition of some at Jerusalem to the acceptance of Gentile converts without circumcision. Although the famous meeting at Jerusalem *ca.* AD 49 settled that question in the affirmative (Acts 15:1-29; Galatians 2:1-10), it did not settle the issue of relations between Jewish and Gentile Christians. Subsequent confrontation at Antioch involved Peter, Paul, and adherents of James (the leader of the Jerusalem church); and apparently a conservative attitude toward the Jewish heritage won out—a position more conservative than Paul's (Galatians 2:11-14).

Matt reflects the situation decades later. Despite the Gospel's echoes of a strongly Jewish-Christian background, there are amid the Christians addressed many Gentiles, perhaps constituting the majority. Although Jesus came only for the lost sheep of the House of Israel (10:5-6; 15:24), by the will of the risen Christ the mission had succeeded in making disciples of all nations (28:19); and these Gentiles had been more willing to listen than those who were originally the tenants of God's vineyard (21:41). In the Gospel's outlook this change from Jews to Gentiles seems to be God's punishment because of the rejection and crucifixion of Jesus (27:25), but Matt also stresses that the Jewish heritage must be preserved. Most scholars, Catholic and

[14] The general outline is important for seeing how individual pericopes fit into the whole. In the outlines and my comments I draw on material in my *Introduction to the New Testament* (New York: Doubleday, 1997). I am grateful to the publisher for permission to reuse. That work would supply readers with much longer treatments of the Gospels than I can provide here.

Chapter 2. Matthew

Protestant, agree that the evangelist was not Matthew, one of the Twelve Apostles and an eyewitness of Jesus' ministry, but a Jewish convert of the second or third generation,[15] probably a scribe, "instructed in the kingdom of heaven . . . a householder who brings out of his treasure new things and old" (13:52). The ideal of preserving the old wineskins as well as the new wine (9:17) illustrates the Matthean Jesus' attitude toward the Law. Every small letter and even part of a letter of the Law (jot and tittle) are to remain (5:18), but only as radically interpreted by Jesus: "You have heard it said [by God to Moses], but I say to you" (5:21, etc.). Such new Christian interpretations were more liberal than the views prevalent in the emerging rabbinic Judaism of the last decades of the 1st century—rabbis who were in some ways the heirs of the Pharisees of Jesus' time. Accordingly, the Gospel contains a fierce critique of the Pharisees, lapsing at times into polemical exaggeration. Although these Jewish teachers may have succeeded to the chair of Moses (23:2-3), they are insulted as "hypocrites" (23:13, etc.). Probably the antagonism stems in part from the fact that the mixed Jewish and Gentile Christians addressed in the Gospel were no longer welcome in the local Jewish synagogues. This alienation is reflected in the description "their synagogues" (Matt 4:23, etc.) and in Jesus' warning about the fate of some of those whom he sends out: "You will scourge some of them in *your* synagogues" (23:34). A separate Christian entity or even institution had emerged, namely, the enduring church of Jesus founded on Peter as the chief representative of those who proclaimed Jesus as the Messiah, the Son of God (16:18).

To enable Jesus to speak to Christians living in this context Matthew composed a masterful account of the one who was the visible presence of "God with us" (1:23). Having before him what Mark had written as "The gospel of Jesus Christ,"

[15] A minority thinks the evangelist was a Gentile. Whether he was Jew or Gentile, it is customary for scholars to keep calling this unknown figure "Matthew." The same custom of traditional name will be followed in regard to the other evangelists in the subsequent Chapters.

Christ in the Gospels of the Ordinary Sundays

Matthew incorporated about 80 percent of that work into his own.[16] Mark had concentrated on what Jesus had done, and to fill out the picture Matthew added a collection of Jesus' teachings (found also in Luke and drawn from a tradition that we call Q). That material he organized into five magnificent sermons, beginning with the Sermon on the Mount, thus contributing in a unique way to the image of Jesus the lawgiver and teacher of the New Covenant, one greater than Moses, who would guide all, Jew and Gentile alike, to God. In a number of places, by a formula such as "This happened in order to fulfill . . . ," Matthew calls attention to how what happens in the Gospel matches OT expectations; and the care with which the appropriate OT text is chosen suggests that meticulous, almost bookish study of the Christian tradition has already begun. Finally, Matthew incorporates in his portrait of Jesus narrative material found in no other Gospel, as seen, for instance, in the accounts of Jesus' infancy and death. Characteristic of this material are vivid imagination (dreams, plotting), extraordinary heavenly and earthly phenomena (angelic interventions, sign of a heavenly star, earthquakes), and an unusual amount of scriptural influence. Many would suggest that here Matthew is tapping a vein of popular folk tradition about Jesus, less formal than material derived from preaching. To all this the evangelist has brought his own writing skill, developed theology, and remarkable pedagogical sense, so that the Gospel presented first in the NT and the liturgy has become the most influential.

Various methods of dividing Matt have been proposed, but the outline given on an accompanying page can help for a basic understanding.

---

[16] With changes of style and emphasis: Overall Matthew writes with more polish and avoids descriptions of Jesus or the disciples that might appear insufficiently reverent.

Chapter 2. Matthew

Outline of the Gospel according to Matthew

1:1–2:23   **Introduction: Origin and Infancy of Jesus the Messiah:**
1. The who and how of Jesus' identity (1:1-25);
2. The where and whence of Jesus' birth and destiny (2:1-23).

3:1–7:29   **Part One: Proclamation of the Kingdom:**
1. Narrative: Ministry of JBap, baptism of Jesus, the temptations, beginning of the Galilean ministry (3:1–4:25);
2. Discourse: Sermon on the Mount (5:1–7:29).

8:1–10:42   **Part Two: Ministry and Mission in Galilee:**
1. Narrative mixed with short dialogue: Nine miracles consisting of healings, calming a storm, exorcism (8:1–9:38);
2. Discourse: Mission Sermon (10:1-42).

11:1–13:52   **Part Three: Questioning of and Opposition to Jesus:**
1. Narrative setting for teaching and dialogue: Jesus and JBap, woes on disbelievers, thanksgiving for revelation, Sabbath controversies and Jesus' power, Jesus' family (11:1–12:50);
2. Discourse: Sermon in Parables (13:1-52).

13:53–18:35   **Part Four: Christology and Ecclesiology:**
1. Narrative mixed with much dialogue: Rejection at Nazareth, feeding the 5,000 and walking on the water, controversies with the Pharisees, healings, feeding the 4,000, Peter's confession, first passion prediction, transfiguration, second passion prediction (13:53–17:27);
2. Discourse: Sermon on the Church (18:1-35).

19:1–25:46   **Part Five: Journey to and Ministry in Jerusalem:**
1. Narrative mixed with much dialogue: Teaching, judgment parables, third passion prediction, entry to Jerusalem, cleansing the Temple, clashes with authorities (19:1–23:39);
2. Discourse: Eschatological Sermon (24:1–25:46).

26:1–28:20   **Climax: Passion, Death, and Resurrection:**
1. Conspiracy against Jesus, Last Supper (26:1-29);
2. Arrest, Jewish and Roman trials, crucifixion, death (26:30–27:56);
3. Burial, guard at the tomb, opening of tomb, bribing of the guard, resurrection appearances (27:57–28:20).

Christ in the Gospels of the Ordinary Sundays

On the 3d Sunday of the Ordinary Time the Lectionary begins the consecutive reading of Matt with 4:12. In order to
understand the Jesus who is described there, let me devote the
following three paragraphs to what Matt 1:1–4:11 has already
told us, some of which has been read in the liturgy.

The Lectionary separates off Matt's infancy narrative (chapters 1–2) for use in the last week of Advent and Christmas. I
have already treated these chapters in two other books in this
series: *A Coming Christ in Advent* and *An Adult Christ at Christmas*. What should be remembered from that material is that the
evangelist wanted the Gospel account of Jesus' ministry (which
begins with Part One: 3:1–7:29) to be introduced by a survey of
Israel's history (the genealogy) and a replay of the story of how
Joseph brought Israel to Egypt to save it, and how Moses was
spared when the wicked ruler (OT: Pharaoh; NT: Herod) tried
to kill the male children. What God does in Jesus is new but
was substantially anticipated by what God did in and for Israel.
The unique Son of God who will come from Galilee to be baptized is the kingly Messiah of the House of David.

Matt's introductory presentation of JBap (3:1-12) was read in
the liturgy on the 2d Sunday of Advent. In that passage Matt
was following Mark's opening pattern, with JBap preaching in
the wilderness as Isaiah had foretold and baptizing with water
in anticipation of the one who would baptize with the Holy
Spirit. What might especially be noted for our present purposes
is Matt's insertion of JBap's condemnation of the Pharisees and
Sadducees and his threats of destruction (3:7-12). The evangelist
thus makes explicable their rejection of JBap, to be reported in
21:25-26, and also Jesus' hostility toward them. A noteworthy
Matthean addition in the account of Jesus' baptism (3:13-17) is
designed to deal with an implicit christological problem: JBap
recognizes that Jesus who is greater should be doing the baptizing, but Jesus accepts baptism from JBap as part of God's
salvific plan related to the kingdom ("righteousness"; see 6:33).

Chapter 2. Matthew

21

Throughout the Gospel this evangelist will be very careful of anything that could detract from the uniquely high status of Jesus.

The testing/temptation of Jesus after forty days and forty nights in the desert (4:1-11—not read in the liturgy until the 1st Sunday of Lent in Year A) serves a double purpose. First, these temptations, partially shaped from the kinds of testing Jesus underwent during the ministry, illustrate the ways in which the proclamation of God's kingdom might have been diverted, so that it would have become a kingdom according to the standards of this world.[17] Second, they prepare us for the continued opposition of Satan, who regards Jesus' proclamation of the kingdom as a threat to his own power and kingdom. The temptations are prognostic of eventual victory; for after Jesus has demonstrated that he is the Son of God who completely serves God's will, the devil departs and angels wait on Jesus (4:11).

As we now turn to the main concern of this book, the reading of Matt on Sundays, let me emphasize that what I present below is too brief to constitute even a mini-commentary. It is meant to provide an overview so that the Sunday pericopes can be seen in context and interpreted in the sequence in which Matt presents them. A helpful way of reading it would be to take what follows section by section (indicated by indented headings) and to reread that section each Sunday covered therein before concentrating on the individual pericope.

JESUS BEGINS GALILEE MINISTRY; CALLS DISCIPLES; SERMON ON THE MOUNT (4:12–7:29; SUNDAYS 3–9)
The consecutive reading of Matt begins on the 3d SUNDAY of the Ordinary Time with 4:12-23, where Jesus goes to Galilee, begins

---

[17] For instance, using miraculous power for personal convenience (stones to bread) or for aggrandizement (showing off from the Temple pinnacle), or for domination (all the kingdoms of the earth). Jesus' refusals to have his goals distorted are all phrased in quotations from Deuteronomy 6–8, where, during the forty-year testing of Israel in the wilderness, God spoke through Moses to the people, who were tempted to rebel against the divine plan by false worship.

Christ in the Gospels of the Ordinary Sundays

his ministry, and calls his first four disciples to become fishers of "men" (= people). To this sequence taken from Mark, Matt adds a geographical precision relating Capernaum to Zebulun and Naphtali, which prepares for a citation[18] from Isaiah 8:23–9:1 that speaks of "Galilee of the Gentiles." Once more Matt has in view his mixed congregation with many Gentiles. The summary of the spread of the Gospel (4:24-25), although drawn from Mark, makes a special point that his fame went out "through all Syria," perhaps because the Gospel was written there.

The Sermon on the Mount (5:1–7:29) is Matt's greatest composition. It weaves together Q material with uniquely Matthean passages into a harmonious masterpiece of ethical and religious teaching. More than any other teacher of morality, the Matthean Jesus instructs with divine power and authority, and by this empowerment makes possible a new existence. There are parallels between Moses and the Matthean Jesus. The OT conveyer of divine revelation encountered God on a mountain; the NT revealer speaks to his disciples on a mountain (Matt 5:1-2). For Christians, next to the Ten Commandments as an expression of God's will, the eight Beatitudes (5:3-12; SUNDAY 4) have been revered for expressing succinctly the values on which Jesus placed priority. In the comparable Lucan passage (6:20-23) there are only four beatitudes (phrased more concretely: "you who are poor . . . hungry now . . . weep now . . . when people hate you"); and it is likely that Matt has added spiritualizing phrases ("poor *in spirit* . . . hunger and thirst *for righteousness*") and four spiritual beatitudes (meek, merciful, pure in heart, peacemakers). Seemingly Matt's community has some people who are not physically poor and hungry; and the evangelist gives assurance that there was an outreach of Jesus to them as well, if they have attitudes attuned to the kingdom. Jesus

[18] This is a citation using the formula "That what was spoken by the prophet Isaiah might be fulfilled." Matt has ten to fourteen such formula citations (more than the other Gospels put together); they reflect the evangelist's careful study of the Scriptures.

Chapter 2. Matthew

teaches these beatitudes to the disciples who are to be the salt of the earth and the light of the world (5:13-16; SUNDAY 5).

The ethics of the new lawgiver (5:17-48; SUNDAYS 6–7) constitutes a remarkable section, not only for the way it has shaped the Christian understanding of Jesus' values but also for its implicit christology. In presenting God's demand the Matthean Jesus does not dispense with the Law but asks for a deeper observance that gets to the reason why its demands were formulated, namely, to be "perfect as your heavenly Father is perfect" (5:48). The polemics of Matt's time are illustrated by the evaluation of Jesus' righteousness as exceeding that of the scribes and Pharisees. In the series of six slightly variant "You have heard it said . . . but I say to you" clauses, Jesus dares explicitly to modify or correct what God said through Moses. He makes the demand of the Law more penetrating (e.g., by prohibiting not only killing but anger, not only adultery but lust); he forbids altogether what the Law allows (no divorce, no oath); and he turns from the Law to its opposite (not retaliation [Deuteronomy 19:21] but generosity to offenders; not hating enemies [Deuteronomy 7:2] but loving them). In other words the Matthean Jesus, speaking more confidently than any 1st-century rabbi, implies that he is more authoritative than Moses and seems to legislate with all the assurance of the God of Sinai.

In 6:1-18 (not read on Sunday but on Ash Wednesday) Jesus reshapes the exercise of piety: almsgiving, prayer, fasting. His warnings are not against pious practices but against ostentation. The Lord's Prayer, taken from Q, has been shaped by Matt partially along the familiar lines of synagogue prayer, for example, the reverential "Our Father who are in heaven." The organization into six petitions reflects Matt's love of order. The first three, "May your name be hallowed, may your kingdom come, may your will come about on earth as in heaven," are different ways of asking God to bring about the kingdom definitively. (This prayer then, at least in its earlier emphasis, was not far from the tone of *Maranatha*—"Come, Lord Jesus" [1 Corinthians 16:22; Revelation 22:20].) The second three deal with the fate of

Christ in the Gospels of the Ordinary Sundays

the petitioners as they anticipate that future moment. The coming of the kingdom will involve the heavenly banquet, and so they ask a share of its food (bread); it will involve judgment, and so they ask forgiveness, assessed by the criterion of forgiving others that Matt emphasizes (25:45); it will involve a dangerous struggle with Satan, and so they ask to be delivered from the apocalyptic trial and the Evil One.[19]

There follow further instructions on behavior for the kingdom (6:19–7:27, with 6:24-34 read on SUNDAY 8, and 7:21-27 on SUNDAY 9). At our time when a consumer society is very concerned with the best in clothes and food and when a great deal of energy is put into being sure that we have financial security for the future, the Matthean Jesus' challenge not to worry about what to eat, or to wear, or about tomorrow may be even more biting than in his own time. The praise of those who hear Jesus' words (7:24-27) as building a well-founded house almost constitutes a judgment against those who reject him. The "When Jesus finished these words" formula terminates the sermon, with the accompanying theme of astonishment at the authority of Jesus' teaching.

MINISTRY IN GALILEE; MISSION SERMON (8:1–10:42; SUNDAYS 10–13)

There now follow in chapters 8 and 9 of Matt three sets of three miracles constituting a total of nine (healings, calming a storm, exorcism), interspersed with dialogues, mostly pertaining to discipleship. Only 9:9-13 is read in the Lectionary (SUNDAY 10): There in an adaptation of the Marcan call of Levi, Jesus calls Matthew, a tax collector. (That change of name had a role in

---

[19] English-speaking Protestants are familiar with an ending of the Lord's Prayer, "For thine is the kingdom, and the power, and the glory, for ever. Amen," which the King James translators took from inferior Greek manuscripts. Although not an original part of Matt, it was a very early liturgical expansion. In the "Communion" section of the Roman Catholic Mass, the Lord's Prayer is followed by a short invocation and then a form of that ancient ascription: "For the kingdom, the power, and the glory are yours, now and forever."

Chapter 2. Matthew

attributing this Gospel to Matthew.) Tax collectors often abused their role by oppressive exaction, but Jesus justifies his selection by announcing that he has come to call sinners, not the righteous. These chapters close with Jesus' observation that the harvest of the crowds needs laborers (9:35-38), and in turn that leads to Jesus' addressing the laborers whom he has chosen.

The Mission Sermon (10:1-42) is set in the context of Jesus' sending out the "disciples" with authority over unclean spirits and the power to heal—Jesus is giving them his power to proclaim the kingdom (compare 10:7 with 4:17). Three portions of the sermon are read in the Sunday Lectionary. In the introductory part of 10:1-8 (SUNDAY 11) Matt stops to recite the names of the Twelve "Apostles,"[20] thus relating the mission of the twelve disciples in the midst of the ministry to the apostolic sending after the resurrection (28:16-20). Even before he was crucified Jesus knew that others had a role to play in spreading the good news of the kingdom; and the directives in the sermon have an ongoing force in the Christian mission known to Matt's readers. In 10:5-6 Jesus warns them not to go to the Gentiles and the Samaritans but to "the lost sheep of the house of Israel." This probably reflects the history of Matthean Christianity, where there was at first almost exclusively a mission to the Jews and only later a mission to the Gentiles.[21] The Matthean Jesus anticipates the kind of persecution that will greet the postresurrectional apostles, but they are assured divine care (10:26-33; SUNDAY 12). And their acknowledging Jesus in the face of hostile persecutors guarantees that Jesus will acknowledge them before

[20] It may be observed that Luke 6:13-15 and Acts 1:13 present a list of the Twelve that differs from that in Matt 10:2-4 (and Mark 3:16-19) in one of the last four names: Thaddaeus in Mark and most manuscripts of Matt; Lebbaeus in some Western manuscripts of Matt; Judas (Jude) in Luke-Acts. Apparently by the time the evangelists wrote, amidst agreement about Jesus' choice of the Twelve, recollection of the minor members was uncertain.

[21] Matt 28:19: "Make disciples of all nations." The mixing of two time periods in the sermon is easily recognizable: Although Jesus forbids the disciples to go near the Gentiles, he speaks of their being put on trial by Gentile as well as Jewish authorities.

Christ in the Gospels of the Ordinary Sundays

his heavenly Father. Jesus warns that following him requires difficult choices in relation both to family ties and life (10:37-42; SUNDAY 13), but generosity will bring a generous reward. The ending of the sermon highlights the salvific importance of the mission: Receiving the missionaries is receiving Jesus, and receiving him is receiving the God who sent him.

QUESTIONING OF AND OPPOSITION TO JESUS; THE SERMON IN PARABLES (11:1–13:52; SUNDAYS 14–17)

Two chapters (11:1–12:50), largely of teaching and dialogue, precede the next great sermon. Set in the context of Jesus moving about in Galilean cities, they concern a medley of subjects: Jesus and JBap, woes on disbelievers, thanksgiving for revelation, Sabbath controversies, and Jesus' family. (Although we have not been told that Jesus' disciples returned from their mission, they are with him in 12:2,49.) The imprisoned JBap has heard of the deeds of the Messiah, and so 11:4-6 explains that Jesus is the kind of Messiah prophesied by Isaiah.[22] Then (11:7-15) Jesus reveals that JBap is more than a prophet: He is the angelic messenger sent by God to lead Israel to the Promised Land (Exodus 23:20) and the Elijah sent to prepare Israel for God's action (Malachi 3:1,23-24). JBap accomplished this by having prepared the way for Jesus, thus becoming the greatest human being ever born before the kingdom of heaven came. Apocalyptic struggle introduces the full coming of the kingdom, and the imprisonment and ultimately the execution of JBap are marks of that. Having spoken about his own identity and that of JBap, in 11:16-19 Jesus criticizes sharply "this generation" for being willing to accept neither.

Next the Lectionary skips to 11:25-30 (SUNDAY 14; also the feast of the Sacred Heart), where Jesus speaks in the style of divine Wisdom by thanking the Father for revelation given to

[22] Matt 11:2-11, describing how the imprisoned JBap sent envoys to Jesus to ask if he is the one to come, is read on the 3d Sunday of Advent in Year A as part of the liturgical motif that JBap is a figure preparatory for the coming of Jesus on Christmas.

Chapter 2. Matthew

those who are childlike, including those who do not count in this world. This jubilant cry, drawn from Q, represents a type of high christology very close to what we find in John's Gospel, where Jesus calls himself the divine Son to whom the Father has given all things (John 3:35; 5:22,26-27); no one knows God except that Son (1:18; 14:9) who reveals the Father to the chosen (17:6). And in the "Come to me" invitation to the heavy-laden (Matt 11:28-30), Jesus (like God in Exodus 33:14 and Wisdom in Sirach 6:23-31) promises rest to those who take on themselves the obligations of the kingdom. These are among the sweetest words ever attributed to Jesus—words that make intelligible Paul's appreciation for "the meekness and gentleness of Christ" (2 Corinthians 10:1).

The Lectionary omits the rest of chapter 11 and all of chapter 12, which set Jesus' teaching in a series of controversies. They have a christological import, since Jesus declares that his presence is greater than the Temple, that the Son of Man is lord of the Sabbath, and that he is acting in the spirit of the prophets. Ominously, the Pharisees react by planning to destroy Jesus. This leads into the Sermon in Parables (13:1-52), which structurally is the center of the Gospel and (since Jesus is not likely to have spoken seven or eight parables on one occasion) illustrates Matthew's pedagogical interest in bringing together like material. The parables serve as a varied commentary on the rejection of Jesus by the Pharisees in the two preceding chapters. The sermon opens with the parable of the sower and its interpretation (13:1-23; SUNDAY 15), which emphasizes the different kinds of obstacles and failures encountered by the proclamation of the kingdom. The weeds among the wheat and its interpretation (13:24-43; SUNDAY 16) seems to move to another level of concern. After the proclamation has won adherents to ("sons of") the kingdom, they will be living together in the world with evil people (who are "sons of" the Evil One). Why not eliminate the evil? Unfortunately that could lead to the good being pulled out as well, and so the separation has to be left to a future judgment by the Son of Man. The Matthean Jesus tends to give

Christ in the Gospels of the Ordinary Sundays

erring Christian community members a time to mend their ways (see 18:15-17). The paired parables of the mustard seed and the leaven (Matt 13:31-33) illustrate the present small beginnings of the kingdom and its great future by using examples of extraordinary growth familiar respectively to a man and to a woman. The paired parables of the hidden treasure and the pearl of great price (13:44-46; SUNDAY 17) stress the great value of the kingdom and the necessity of taking the once-for-all opportunity to gain it, even if that requires selling off everything else. The dragnet and its interpretation (13:47-50) once more postpones the separation of the good and bad in the kingdom till the close of the age. The sermon ends with a summary parable of the householder and the new and old treasure (13:51-52). Those who have understood the parables are like a trained scribe who appreciates the new revelation in Jesus and the old revelation in Moses. The evangelist probably considered himself in this light.

CHRISTOLOGY AND ECCLESIOLOGY (13:53–18:35; SUNDAYS 18–24)

A great variety of subjects are treated in the mixed narrative and dialogue (13:53–17:27) that precedes the next sermon: rejection at Nazareth, feeding the 5,000 and walking on the water, controversies with the Pharisees, healings, feeding the 4,000, Peter's confession, first passion prediction, transfiguration, second passion prediction. In 13:10-11 Jesus had said that he spoke in parables because the disciples were to know the mysteries of the kingdom of heaven; accordingly, in what now follows Jesus turns his main attention to the disciples from whom the church will develop, especially to Peter the rock on whom the church will be built. The rejection at Nazareth (13:54-58) helps to explain why Jesus must concentrate on his disciples, since even his townspeople do not accept him.[23] The lack of faith at Nazareth is followed by an account of how Herod killed JBap

[23] Matt shows greater reverence for Jesus and his family than does the parallel in Mark 6:1-6: He does not report that Jesus was a carpenter or was a prophet without honor "among his own relatives." (Matt's substitution of "son

Chapter 2. Matthew

(14:1-12) and was superstitiously uneasy about Jesus. In an attempt to get away from Herod Jesus withdraws to a lonely place where he feeds the 5,000 and subsequently walks on the water (14:13-33; SUNDAYS 18–19). There are different layers of theological emphasis in these miracles: They echo miracles of Moses (the manna and walking dry-shod through the Red Sea) and of the prophet Elisha (2 Kings 4:42-44); also the loaves miracle anticipates eucharistic feeding, and the walking on the water is a type of theophany illustrating Jesus' divine identity (note the "I am" ["It is I"] in Matt 14:27). The end of the walking-on-the-water scene is remarkable in Matt; for in 14:33 the disciples, instead of failing to understand as in Mark 6:52, worship Jesus as "Son of God." Most significant is the scene peculiar to Matt where Jesus invites Peter to come to him on the water, and as Peter begins to sink, Jesus helps him (14:28-31). This is the first of three instances of special Petrine material in Matt. Peter's impetuousness, the inadequacy of his faith, and Jesus' individual care to lead Peter further are quite characteristic. As a man of little faith who would sink unless the Lord saved him, Peter is representative of the other disciples; their faith and his in the Son of God gains strength from Jesus' powerful helping hand.

The debate with the Pharisees and scribes from Jerusalem over what defiles (15:1-20) leads Jesus to condemn blind guides who will be rooted out. Moving on to Tyre and Sidon, Jesus heals the daughter of the Canaanite woman (15:21-28; SUNDAY 20), a story resembling the healing of the centurion's servant boy in 8:5-13. At the Sea of Galilee we are told of the second multiplication of loaves, namely, for the 4,000 (15:32-39). While this may be a preaching variant of the earlier story, the repetition has the effect of emphasizing Jesus' power.

Amid hostile confrontations Jesus rejects the disbelieving request for a sign: The Pharisees and Sadducees cannot interpret the

---

of a carpenter" for Mark's "carpenter" gave rise to the artistic custom of depicting Joseph as a carpenter.)

Christ in the Gospels of the Ordinary Sundays

already present signs of the times. Criticizing his disciples as people who have little faith for they have not fully understood the bread miracles, Jesus warns them against the leaven or teaching of the Pharisees and Sadducees,[24] whom he equates with an evil and adulterous generation. Yet Jesus' disciples have considerable faith, for in 16:13-20 (SUNDAY 21) Peter confesses that Jesus is the Son of the living God—a revelation from the Father in heaven, not a matter of human reasoning ("flesh and blood"). The revelation to Paul of Jesus' divine sonship is phrased in almost the same language (Galatians 1:16). If that revelation constituted Paul an apostle, this one constitutes Peter the rock on which Jesus will build his church, a church that even the gates of hell (probably Satanic destructive power) will not prevail against. The OT background of Peter's acknowledgment of Jesus as the Davidic Messiah, the Son of God, is the prophecy of 2 Samuel 7: David's descendant will reign after him and God will treat him as a son. That promise was provoked by David's desire to build a house or temple for God, and so Jesus' promise to build a church on Peter, who acknowledges him as the fulfillment of the promise to David, is not illogical. Isaiah 22:15-25 describes the establishment of Eliakim as the new prime minister of King Hezekiah of Judah: God places on his shoulder "the *key* of the House of David; he shall *open* . . . and he shall *shut*." The italicized words are echoed in Matt 16:19 as Jesus gives to Peter the keys of the kingdom, so that whatever he binds/looses on earth is bound/loosed in heaven. Matt's picture of the exaltation of Peter does not eliminate Jesus' subsequent chastisement of Peter as Satan (16:21-23; SUNDAY 22), who thinks on a human level because he does not accept the notion of Jesus' suffering in the first of three similar predictions of the passion. This sobering correction leads into directives (16:24-27) to the disciples both about the suffering required for discipleship and about future glory when the Son of Man comes.

[24] This not easily reconcilable with 23:2-3, where Jesus says that his disciples are to practice and observe whatever the scribes and the Pharisees tell them because they sit on the chair of Moses.

Chapter 2. Matthew

The account of the transfiguration (17:1-9; 2d Sunday of Lent in Year A) is another step in the Matthean christological sequence pertaining to divine sonship that runs from the angelic annunciation to Joseph that the child was conceived through the Holy Spirit (1:20), through God's revelation about "my Son" (2:15), to the voice from heaven at the baptism speaking of "my beloved Son" (3:17), to the disciples' recognition after the walking on the water (14:33), culminating in Peter's confession (16:16).

The rest of chapter 17 is not read in the Sunday Lectionary. Unfortunately that means the omission of another special Matthean Petrine scene centered on the (Temple?) tax (17:24-27),[25] where Peter is the intermediary in teaching Christians to avoid public offense by paying the tax on a voluntary basis and thus to be peaceable citizens (see Romans 13:6-7; 1 Peter 2:13-16). His role is all the more important if on the Gospel level Matthew is dealing with a problem faced by Christians after Peter was dead.

The Sermon on the Church (18:1-35) gives to a collection of ethical teaching, much of it once addressed to Jesus' disciples, a perspective that makes it strikingly suited to an established church, the type of church that only Matt has Jesus mention (16:18). Matt connects ecclesiology and christology, for the apostles are to interpret and teach all that Jesus commanded (28:20). Although a structured church is the context in which the tradition and memory of Jesus are preserved, Matt recognizes a danger: Any structure set up in this world tends to take its values from the other structures that surround it. This chapter is meant to insure that those values do not smother the values of Jesus. To readers who struggle with church issues today, this may be the most helpful of the five Matthean sermons; and so those who preach might well interpret the *whole* sermon, even though the Sunday Lectionary includes only two excerpts from it. The peculiarly Matthean instructions in 18:15-20 (Sunday 23) are clearly

[25] It reflects oral tradition, with the finding of the stater coin in the fish's mouth adding almost a folkloric touch.

Christ in the Gospels of the Ordinary Sundays

adapted to a church situation, for after the unsuccessful efforts of individuals to win over a reprobate, a report is to be made to the "church" (=local community, unlike the use of "church" in 16:18). The process is designed to prevent too early and frequent use of authority—a danger in any structured community. The quarantine of the recalcitrant reprobate in 18:17 "as a Gentile and tax-collector" sounds very definitive, reinforced by the power to bind and loose in 18:18. Yet we must remember that Matt's community was a mixed one of Jews and Gentiles, and that Jesus' final instruction was to go out to the Gentiles and teach them (28:19). Moreover, Jesus had shown a particular interest in a tax collector named Matthew, inviting him to follow (9:9; 10:3). Therefore, the repudiated Christian may still be the subject of outreach and concern. In 18:21-22 (SUNDAY 24) Peter is once more a figure of authority getting instruction from Jesus on how he should act. Although he is being a bit "legalistic" in trying to find out how often he should forgive, his offer is quite generous—except for the family circle few people forgive someone seven times. Jesus gives a remarkable answer: seventy-seven, that is, an infinite number of times (cf. Genesis 4:24). Christian forgiveness, then, is to imitate the unlimited range of God's forgiveness, as is confirmed by the eloquent parable of the unforgiving servant (18:23-35), which invokes divine judgment on those who refuse to forgive. All this has a very real application in church life, for the number of people who turn away from the church where they have not found forgiveness is legion. Overall, to the extent that churches listen to Jesus speaking to his disciples in this chapter, they will keep his spirit alive instead of memorializing him. Then Matt 18:20 will be fulfilled: "Where two or three are gathered in my name, there am I in the midst of them."

JOURNEY TO AND MINISTRY IN JERUSALEM (19:1–25:46; SUNDAYS 25–34)

Leading to the next sermon is a section with vivid narrative mixed with much dialogue (19:1–23:39): teaching, judgment parables, third passion prediction, entry to Jerusalem, cleansing

Chapter 2. Matthew

the Temple, clashes with authorities. After Jesus has revealed his intention to found his church and has given instructions about the attitudes that must characterize it, he goes up to Jerusalem, where his predictions about the death and resurrection of the Son of Man will be fulfilled.

The whole of chapter 19 is omitted in the Sunday Lectionary, which moves directly to the parable of the workers in the vineyard (20:1-16; SUNDAY 25), which is peculiar to Matt. The payment begins with the last hired workers and moves to the first hired, so that it may be seen by those who worked all day long that all are paid the same. The parable illustrates that God's gracious giving is not determined by what is earned—a Matthean example of a major Pauline emphasis.

The entry into Jerusalem (21:1-11) constitutes the reading for the procession with palms on Passion (Palm) Sunday in Year A. It is highlighted by citations of Isaiah 62:11 and Zechariah 9:9 that stress the meekness and peacefulness of the messianic king.[26] The Sunday Lectionary skips over the cleansing of the Temple, the cursing and withering of the fig tree, and the challenge to Jesus' authority by the priests and the elders, answered in terms of JBap (Matt 21:12-27). The peculiarly Matthean parable of the two sons (21:28-32; SUNDAY 26) compares the authorities to the son who says he will obey the father but does not. Jesus fashions a highly polemic contrast: Tax collectors and harlots who believed JBap will enter the kingdom of God before the authorities. The sharpness of the judgment continues in the parable of the wicked tenants (21:33-43; SUNDAY 27), for afterwards in verses 43,45 the chief priests and the Pharisees understand themselves to be the target of the warning that the kingdom of God will be taken away and given to a nation that will produce fruits. Matt is thinking of the church composed of Jews and Gentiles who believe in Jesus. The parable of the marriage feast (22:1-14; SUNDAY 28), seemingly adapted from Q, is

[26] Famously illogical is the Matthean combination in 21:7 of ass and colt (originally meant as parallel designations of one animal) so that Jesus sat "on them."

Christ in the Gospels of the Ordinary Sundays

another instance of the rejection of the leaders. Those invited first by the king are unworthy and do not come; and since they kill the servants sent with the invitation, the king sends his troops and destroys their city. The once independent parable about the man without a wedding garment, which has been added as an ending, deals with a reality that Matt knows well: Into the church have been brought both bad and good, so that those who have accepted the initial call have to face further judgment. Those Christians who are not worthy will suffer the same fate as those who formerly had the kingdom but were not worthy to keep it (cf. 8:11-12). Thus in none of these three parables is it simply a question of the replacement of Israel by the church or of Jews by Gentiles; the issue for Matt is the replacement of the unworthy in Judaism (especially the leaders) by a community of Jews and Gentiles who have come to believe in Jesus and have worthily responded to his demands for the kingdom.

There now follows a series of three trap questions: taxes for Caesar proposed by Pharisees and Herodians (Matt 22:15-21; SUNDAY 29); the resurrection proposed by Sadducees (22:23-33); the great commandment proposed by a Pharisee lawyer (22:34-40; SUNDAY 30). These are followed by a question proposed by Jesus to the Pharisees about the Messiah as David's son (22:41-46; not read in the Sunday Lectionary). Serving as a bridge to the last great discourse, Jesus' denunciation of the scribes and Pharisees (23:1-36) is an extraordinary Matthean construction. Only 23:1-12 is read in the Lectionary (SUNDAY 31), perhaps because the material is so hostile. Altogether Jesus delivers seven "woes" against their casuistry—woes that function almost as the antitheses of the Beatitudes in chapter 5. Although the seven woes are portrayed as Jesus' critiques of the Jewish leaders of his time, Matt's readers would probably hear them as critiques of synagogue leaders in their time over a half century later. (And Christians today should hear them as a critique not of Jews but of what generally happens in established religion and thus applicable to behavior in Christianity.) For the Christians

Chapter 2. Matthew

of Matt's church the crucifixion of Jesus would have sharpened the tone of such polemic, and "Amen, I say to you, all these things will come on this generation" (23:36) would have been seen as fulfilled in the capture of Jerusalem and destruction of the Temple in AD 70.

The last of the five great discourses, the Eschatological Sermon (24:1–25:46) deals with the endtimes but is phrased in a type of apocalyptic obscurity that mixes the present time of the Gospel readers with future time. None of chapter 24, with its references to false prophets, desolating sacrilege, and flight in the last times, is read on the Ordinary Sundays.[27] Watchfulness is stressed in the uniquely Matthean parable of the ten virgins (25:1-13; SUNDAY 32). It illustrates well the rule that generally the parables make one point: The uncharitable behavior of the wise virgins in refusing to share their oil with the foolish is not to be imitated, but without that behavior the point of the parable about being ready could not be made. The judgment motif grows stronger in the parable of the talents (25:14-30; SUNDAY 33), where the message is not one of meriting reward but of dedicated and fruitful response by the Christian to God's gift in and through Jesus. The discourse ends with material peculiar to Matt: the enthroned Son of Man judging the sheep and the goats (25:31-46; SUNDAY 34 = Christ the King). Since the Son of Man speaks of God as "my Father," this is the Son of God in the apocalyptic context of the judgment of the whole world. The admirable principle that the verdict is based on the treatment of deprived outcasts is the Matthean Jesus' last warning to his fol-

[27] 24:37-44 constitutes the reading for the 1st Sunday of Advent in Year A. That the last Sunday of the Ordinary Time (Christ the King) and the 1st Sunday of Advent both have Lectionary readings about the return of Christ, the Son of Man, is somehow tied into the idea that we expect the second coming of Christ at the end of time and yet liturgically we also expect a type of second coming at Christmas. If I may be permitted a personal criticism, I think that the use of eschatological readings on the 1st Sunday of Advent is ill advised; we should conclude the eschatological emphasis with Christ the King and prepare for Christmas by a different type of Sunday readings.

Christ in the Gospels of the Ordinary Sundays

lowers and to the church, demanding a very different religious standard both from that of those scribes and Pharisees criticized in chapter 23 and from that of a world that pays more attention to the rich and powerful.

* * *

Passages from the rest of Matt (chapters 26–28), which constitute the passion, burial, and resurrection narratives, are read in Passiontide (particularly Palm Sunday) of Year A and Eastertime. They have already been discussed in this Liturgical Press series of books in *A Crucified Christ in Holy Week* and *A Risen Christ in Eastertime.*

Chapter 2. Matthew

Chapter 3

The Gospel according to Mark
(Liturgical Year B)

This is the Gospel that most scholars think was written earli-est.[28] In formal courses on the Gospels, besides being studied first, Mark gets more attention as the basic Gospel on which Matt and Luke drew. The Sunday Lectionary, however, reads it in the second or B Year. Since it was practically never read on the Sundays in the pre-Vatican II Lectionary, Catholics tend not to be familiar with Mark and often hear it against a background of what they know from Matt. Care has to be taken to point out Marcan distinctiveness and raw narrative power.

INTRODUCTORY OBSERVATIONS

To familiarize readers/hearers with the Gospel that will be used sequentially beginning on the *3d Sunday of the Ordinary Time*, the following details may be of help. Usually scholars date the writing of this most ancient Gospel to between AD 60 and 75, with the most likely date in the range 68–73. By traditional attri-bution going back to the early 2d-century bishop Papias, the au-thor was Mark, the follower and "interpreter" of Peter, usually identified as the John Mark of Acts, whose mother had a house in Jerusalem.[29] Some who reject this attribution suggest that the author may have been an otherwise unknown Christian named Mark.

From the contents the author emerges as a Greek-speaker who was probably not an eyewitness of Jesus' ministry, since he

---

[28] Is this recognized in the order of the sequential Gospel readings in the weekday Mass Lectionary every year: Mark, Matt, Luke?

[29] He accompanied Barnabas and Paul on the "First Missionary Journey" and may have helped Peter and Paul in Rome in the 60s. The name "Mark," how-ever, was common (e.g., Mark Antony); and we cannot be sure that the Mark and John Mark references of the NT all allude to the same man.

Christ in the Gospels of the Ordinary Sundays

makes statements about Palestinian geography that many judge inaccurate. This evangelist (whom I shall continue to call "Mark") drew on preshaped traditions about Jesus (oral and probably written)[30] to produce a compact, effective presentation that began with the words "The gospel of Jesus Christ."[31] Independently, Matthew and Luke were to use Mark's Gospel as a basic guide in composing their works, and so Mark must have been considered a good representative of the way Jesus was preached in the larger church. Papias' reference to Mark as the interpreter of Peter may mean that Mark's Gospel was a distillation from and reorganization of a standard type of preaching that was considered apostolic and therefore associated with Peter, the first of the Twelve.

It is very difficult to discern the community that Mark addressed, but internal evidence points to Gentiles who did not know some basic Jewish customs (7:3-4). Mark's tone and emphases suggest a community that had undergone persecution and failure, so that now they needed encouragement. That plus the fact that there are signs of Latin influences on Mark's Greek has led some modern scholars to accept the 2d-century tradition that Mark was directed to Christians at Rome, for we know that there Christians were persecuted by Nero in AD 64–68.[32]

A popular way to trace development in Mark's thought is found in the Gospel outline on an accompanying page. It posits a major dividing point in Mark 8, approximately halfway through the account of Jesus' ministry. There, after having been consistently rejected and misunderstood despite all he has said and done, Jesus starts to proclaim the necessity of the suffering,

[30] Scholars often claim to have reconstructed the preMarcan sources with great exactitude. It is very dubious that one can do that, and the reconstructions differ greatly.

[31] Mark uses "gospel" in the sense of "message"; but drawing on his title at a later period, Christians began to speak of written "Gospels."

[32] Other proposals center on regions immediately to the north of Palestine (Syria, the northern Transjordan, the Decapolis).

Outline of the Gospel according to Mark

1:1–8:26   **Part One: Ministry of Healing and Preaching in Galilee**:

1. Introduction by JBap; an initial day; controversy at Capernaum (1:1–3:6);
2. Jesus chooses the Twelve and trains them as disciples by parables and mighty deeds; misunderstanding among his Nazareth relatives (3:7–6:6);
3. Sending out the Twelve; feeding 5,000; walking on water; controversy; feeding 4,000; misunderstanding (6:7–8:26).

8:27–16:8   **Part Two: Suffering Predicted; Death in Jerusalem; Resurrection**:

1. Three passion predictions; Peter's confession; the transfiguration; Jesus' teaching (8:27–10:52);
2. Ministry in Jerusalem: Entry; Temple actions and encounters; Eschatological Discourse (11:1–13:37);
3. Anointing, Last Supper, passion, crucifixion, burial, empty tomb (14:1–16:8).

(+16:9–20) The long canonical ending (or **Marcan appendix**) describing resurrection appearances added to the Gospel by a later copyist.

---

death, and resurrection of the Son of Man in God's plan. This development, which serves to reveal the christological identity of Jesus, is meant by Mark to teach a lesson. Readers can learn much about Jesus from the traditions of his parables and mighty deeds; but unless that is intimately combined with the picture of his victory through suffering, they cannot understand him or their own vocation as his followers. This outline should help to dispel any notion that because Mark was an early Gospel it is primitive. Rather, Mark has carefully organized the career of Jesus to convey a message.[33]

By the time Mark wrote, Jesus had been preached as the Christ for several decades. To appreciate what this earliest written portrayal contributed to our Christian heritage, one might

[33] Organization is a characteristic of Stage Three of Gospel Formation, as we saw in Chapter 1, above.

Christ in the Gospels of the Ordinary Sundays

reflect on what we would know about Jesus if we had just the letters of Paul. We would have a magnificent theology about what God has done in Christ, but Jesus would be left almost without a face. Mark gets the honor of having been the first Christian to have painted that "face" and made it part of the enduring good news.

GUIDANCE TO BEGINNING THE SEQUENTIAL USE OF MARK IN THE LECTIONARY

On the 3d Sunday of the Ordinary Time the Lectionary begins the consecutive reading of Mark with 1:14. Since so little precedes that verse in the NT or in the Sunday Lectionary of Year B,[34] one does not have the difficulties presented by Matt and Luke where three and a half chapters precede the beginning of the sequential Lectionary reading of the respective Gospel. Yet the very abruptness of Mark needs to be commented on.[35] Christian audiences in general and Sunday audiences in particular, when they hear that Jesus began a public ministry in Galilee, are accustomed to think of a Jesus conceived by the Holy Spirit of the virgin Mary, born in Bethlehem, reared in Nazareth, and prepared for and baptized by JBap in a relatively lengthy scene—none of which is recounted in Mark. In the briefest way Mark has presented the beginning of the gospel of Jesus Christ[36] as the fulfillment of Malachi 3:1 and Isaiah 40:3

[34] Only: Mark 1:1-8, the appearance of JBap, read on the 2d Sunday of Advent in Year B; Mark 1:7-11, the baptism of Jesus, read on the Feast of the Baptism (=1st Sunday of Ordinary Time). The very brief Marcan account of the testing/tempting of Jesus (1:12-13 + 1:14-15) is read on the 1st Sunday of Lent.

[35] Indeed, Marcan brevity presents a liturgical problem, for this shortest Gospel does not provide enough pericopes or segments to cover all the Sundays in the Ordinary Time. To meet that problem, in mid-summer the Lectionary interrupts its reading of Mark at 6:34 (the beginning of the brief first account of the multiplication of the loaves) and substitutes for five Sundays (17th through 21st) the much longer Johannine account of the multiplication—a disputable decision.

[36] Although Mark 1:1 is often treated as a title, the evangelist may have thought of it as a proclamation. The phrase "Son of God," though supported by major mss., may be a copyist's addition. If genuine it provides an inclusion with the identification

Chapter 3. Mark

about a prophesied messenger (JBap) crying in the wilderness to prepare the way of the Lord. That preparation consists in announcing the one who will baptize with the Holy Spirit, namely, Jesus, who has come from Nazareth and whom a voice from heaven addresses as beloved Son. Then in two verses we are told without any detail that for forty days Jesus was tested by Satan. Presumably Mark's audience knew something more about JBap and about Jesus, but we have no idea whether they knew anything about Jesus' birth or his family (e.g., Joseph is never mentioned by Mark). These differences offer preachers an opportunity to remind Sunday audiences of Gospel differences and of how stories known in one part of the early Christian world may not have been known in other parts.

A worthwhile reflection before beginning the sequential reading of Mark is that, without any angelic announcement of conception, God's voice at the baptism speaking to Jesus of Nazareth, "You are my beloved Son, with you I am well pleased," was enough in Mark's mind for his audience to understand the Gospel story that follows. That voice with its "You are my Son" echoes Psalm 2:7, a psalm used for the coronation of the king of the House of David, and thus points to Jesus as the Messiah. The additional "with you I am well pleased" echoes Isaiah 42:1, which describes the Servant of the Lord as "my chosen one with whom I am pleased," and thus points to Jesus as the Isaian Servant who is to bear the infirmities of many and be led to slaughter for the guilt of all (Isaiah 53:4-10). Thus the Marcan Jesus who begins his ministry has been revealed to the audience both as royal Messiah and as Suffering Servant. And even a two-verse account of the testing of Jesus by Satan (Mark 1:12-13) was enough for Mark's readers/hearers to be aware from the start that Jesus' proclamation of the kingdom or rule of God, which has now come near (i.e., is making itself felt), will encounter major obstacles.

---

of Jesus as "Son of God" by the Roman centurion in 15:39 toward the end—the first believing confession of Jesus under that title in the Gospel.

Christ in the Gospels of the Ordinary Sundays

JESUS BEGINS GALILEE MINISTRY; CALLS DISCIPLES; AN
INITIAL DAY; CONTROVERSY (1:14–3:6; SUNDAYS 3–9)[37]

The reading on the SUNDAY 3 of the Ordinary Time in Year B
starts with 1:14, where, after JBap was arrested, Jesus appears in
Galilee. The first half of Mark describes a ministry of preaching
and powerful deeds (healings, multiplying loaves, calming
storms) and teaching in Galilee and its environs. Although Jesus
attracts great interest, he struggles with demons, encountering
misunderstanding (by his family and, more importantly, by the
Twelve, whom he has chosen to be with him) and hostile rejection (by Pharisees and scribes).

Jesus begins by calling four men to be his followers and "fishers" who will catch people (1:16-20), thus presaging that they will
have a role in the proclamation of Jesus' message. Indeed, the reactions of these disciples will mark major stages in the Gospel.

In describing what appears to be the initial day of Jesus' ministry (1:21-38; SUNDAYS 4–5), Mark familiarizes the readers with
the type of things done in proclaiming the kingdom: teaching in
the Capernaum synagogue with authority, exorcising an unclean spirit (the continued opposition of Satan), healing Simon's
mother-in-law, healing many more diseased and possessed, and
finally seeking a place to pray on the following morning only to
be importuned by his disciples pressing demands on him. Several factors should be noted. Teaching and an exercise of divine
power in healing and driving out demons are united in the
proclamation of the kingdom, implying that the coming of
God's rule is complex. Those who claim to be God's people
must recognize that some of their attitudes stand in the way
and they must change their minds; the presence of evil visible
in human affliction, suffering, and sin must be contravened; and
the demonic must be defeated. Jesus' teaching with authority
and power over the demons stems from his being Son of God.
Yet Mark never describes Jesus being given such authority and

[37] I remind readers of the suggestion on p. 22, above, as to how one might
use the individual sections of my book to accompany the Lectionary passages.

Chapter 3. Mark

power; he simply has it because of who he is. Paradoxically, the unclean spirit that opposes him recognizes that he is the Holy One of God, while the disciples who follow him do not understand him fully despite his teaching and powerful deeds. In 1:34 Jesus forbids the demons to speak "because they knew him." This is the first instance of what scholars call Mark's "Messianic Secret," whereby Jesus seems to hide his identity as the Son of God until it is made apparent after his death on the cross—the full mystery of his person involves suffering and death.

Jesus' activity and controversies are expanded in 1:39–3:6. Moving through the towns of Galilee, proclaiming the kingdom and healing (e.g., a leper in 1:40-45; SUNDAY 6), Jesus seeks to avoid an enthusiasm for the wonderful that could give the wrong understanding. His curing sickness is not meant to arouse astonishment but to teach about the way in which God's rule is to destroy all forms of harmful evil, spiritual and physical. At Capernaum, a town on the Lake of Galilee that has now become Jesus' home, Mark centers five incidents (2:1–3:6) where objections are raised by the scribes and the Pharisees and others to his forgiving sins, to his association with sinners, to the failure of his disciples to fast, and to their and his doing what is not lawful on the Sabbath. The first (2:1-12), the third (2:18-22), and the fourth and fifth (2:23–3:6) are read on SUNDAYS 7, 8, and 9. Clearly Jesus is being presented as one who, on the basis of his own higher authority (2:28: "the Son of Man is lord even of the Sabbath"), does not fit into the religious expectations of his contemporaries—an attitude that gives rise to a plot on the part of the Pharisees and Herodians to destroy him. The proclamation of God's kingdom is opposed not simply by demons but also by human beings.

JESUS CHOOSES THE TWELVE AND TRAINS THEM AS DISCIPLES BY PARABLES AND MIGHTY DEEDS (3:7–6:6; SUNDAYS 10–14)

Mark closes the previous section and begins this section with a summary (3:7-12) showing that Jesus' ministry was attracting

Christ in the Gospels of the Ordinary Sundays

people from an ever-widening region beyond the Galilee of 1:39. Amid this appeal to many, Jesus goes up to the mountain and summons the Twelve (3:13-19), whom he wants to be with him and whom he will send forth (*apostellein*, related to "apostle") to preach. The next chapters show what he does and says when they are with him, presumably to train them for being sent forth (6:7) at the end of this section.

In the sequence 3:20-35 (SUNDAY 10) we encounter a narrative arrangement that scholars acknowledge as a feature of Marcan style (intercalation or "sandwiching"), where Mark initiates an action that requires time to be completed, interrupts it by another scene filling in the time (the meat between the surrounding pieces of bread), and then resumes the initial action, bringing it to a close. Here the action begins with Jesus' relatives, who do not understand this turn of life where he is not even taking the time to eat (3:20-21) and want to bring him back home. The time it requires to move from Nazareth where they are to Jesus' new "home" at Capernaum is filled in by scribes who come from Jerusalem (3:22-30). The relatives' objection "He is beside himself" is matched by the scribes' "He is possessed by Beelzebul," the one expressing radical misunderstanding and the other antagonistic disbelief. At the end of the intercalation, the mother and brothers of Jesus finally arrive (3:31-35); but now that the proclamation of the kingdom has begun, they have been replaced: "Whoever does the will of God is my brother, and sister, and mother." The intermediary scene with scribes from Jerusalem constitutes one of the Marcan Jesus' clearest statements about Satan, whose kingdom opposes the kingdom of God. With the appearance of Jesus the two kingdoms are locked in struggle. The allegorical parable in 3:27 suggests that Satan is the strong one in possession of his house and goods (this world) and that Jesus is the stronger one who has come to bind him and take his possessions away. The unforgivable blasphemy in Mark 3:28-30 is to attribute Jesus' works to an unclean spirit rather than to the Holy Spirit.

The next subsection (4:1-34) is a collection of parables and parabolic sayings pertinent to the kingdom of God, most of

Chapter 3. Mark

them dealing with the growth of seed. Even though Jesus' ministry is centered at Capernaum on the Sea of Galilee, and the setting of these parables is a boat, it seems that the material of Jesus' parables is taken from the villages and farms of the Nazareth hill-country of his youth. There is no real doubt that historically Jesus phrased his teaching in parables. Because they are polyvalent, the particular point of parables takes on coloration from the context in which they are uttered or placed. Scholars have spent much time reconstructing the original context of the parables in Jesus' lifetime and distinguishing it from the subsequent reinterpretations that took place as the parables were preached in the early Christian decades (both of which preGospel contexts are speculative). Yet the only certain context is the placing of the parables in the extant Gospels—the fact that at times the context differs in Mark, Matt, and Luke exemplifies the creative use of tradition by the evangelists for their own pedagogical purposes.

In the present Marcan narrative-sequence three seed parables (the sower and the seed, the seed that grows by itself, and the mustard seed) serve as a commentary on what has been happening in Jesus' proclamation of the kingdom (and anticipate the growing incomprehension by the disciples). In the parable of the sower (not read in the Lectionary of Year B) the emphasis is on the different kinds of soil. The interpretation supplied in Mark for the Gospel audience, even if not derived from Jesus himself, may be close to the original idea: Only some have accepted the proclamation of the kingdom, and even among them there are failures. Yet the next two seed parables (4:26-32; SUNDAY 11) stress that the seed has its own power and will ripen in its own time; it is like the mustard seed with a small beginning and a large growth. Those who heard/read Mark were meant to see these parables as explaining failures and disappointments in their own experience of Christianity and as a sign of hope that ultimately there would be tremendous growth and abundant harvest.

Woven into chapter 4 are comments and parabolic sayings about the "purpose" of the parables. Only 4:33-34 is used in the

Christ in the Gospels of the Ordinary Sundays

Sunday Lectionary (continuing SUNDAY 11), but a full explanation is necessary. In particular, 4:11-12, where Jesus says that
parables are given to those outside in order that they may *not*
see, understand, or be converted, is an offensive text if one does
not understand the biblical approach to divine foresight, where
what has in fact resulted is often presented as God's purpose.
(Thus, in Exodus 7:3-4 God tells Moses of the divine plan to
make Pharaoh obstinate so that he will not listen to Moses—a
hindsight description of the fact that Pharaoh resisted.) Mark is
really describing what he sees as the negative *result* of Jesus'
teaching among his own people, the majority of whom did not
understand and were not converted. Like the symbolic visions
accorded to Daniel in the OT, the parables constituted a "mystery," the interpretation of which was given by God only to the
select (Daniel 2:22,27-28). Others do not understand, and the
mystery becomes a source of destruction. Isaiah 6:9-10, which
foresaw the prophet's failure to convert Judah, was widely used
in the NT to explain the failure of Jesus' followers to convince
most Jews;[38] and Mark employs it here (4:12) in comment on the
parables. That Jesus' purpose (in the proper sense) was not to
obscure is made clear by the sayings about the lamp and the
hidden things in 4:21-23 and also by the summary in 4:33-34
that has Jesus speaking the word to them in parables "to the extent they were able to understand it."

Four miraculous actions follow in 4:35–5:43. These serve to
remind today's readers that the 1st-century worldview was
very different from our own. Many modern scholars dismiss
completely the historicity of the miraculous;[39] others are willing
to accept the healings of Jesus, because they can be related to
the coming of the kingdom as a manifestation of God's mercy,
but reject the historicity of "nature" miracles such as the calm-

[38] Romans 11:7-8; Acts 28:26-27; John 12:37-40.

[39] Almost half Mark's account of the public ministry deals with miracles. The
evangelist describes them as *dynameis* (= acts of power), not using a Greek word
that would call attention to the wondrous, as does English "miracle" (related to
Latin *mirari*, "to wonder at").

Chapter 3. Mark

ing of the storm in Mark 4:35-41 (SUNDAY 12). However, that distinction finds no support in an OT background where God manifests power over all creation. Just as sickness and affliction reflect the kingdom of evil, so also does a dangerous storm; accordingly Jesus rebukes the wind and the sea in 4:39 just as he does a demon in 1:25. (Lest one think this picture impossibly naive, one should note that when a storm causes death and destruction today, people wonder why God has allowed this; they do not vent their anger on a high/low pressure system.) The victory of Jesus over the storm is seen as the action of the stronger one (3:27), whom even the wind and sea obey.

The struggle of Jesus with the demonic is even more dramatic in the healing of the Gerasene madman (5:1-20), which is not read in the Lectionary.[40] The two miracles in 5:21-43 (SUNDAY 13) are another instance of Marcan intercalation ("sandwiching"): Jesus sets out for Jairus' house in 5:21-24 and arrives to raise Jairus' daughter in 5:35-43, while the time in between is filled in by the healing of the woman with the hemorrhage in 5:25-34. In the story of the woman, notice that power is portrayed as a possession of Jesus that can go out from him without his knowing where it goes. The question "Who has touched my clothes?" with the disciples' sarcastic response and the confession of the woman add to the humanity of the drama. Yet, perhaps unintentionally, they give the impression that Jesus did not know all things—that may be why the much shorter form of the story in Matt 9:20-22 omits such details. Jesus' declaration "Your faith has saved you" (Mark 5:34; 10:52) shows that Mark has no mechanical understanding of the miraculous power of Jesus. In the Jairus story we hear of the threesome Peter, James, and John chosen to accompany Jesus. They were the first called of the Twelve; and evidence in Paul and Acts suggests they were the most widely known. The "mighty deed" of Jesus is to

[40] One wonders if this miracle, where Jesus drives out the "Legion" of demons and the need for a place to stay leads to their transferral to pigs, was considered too imaginative.

Christ in the Gospels of the Ordinary Sundays

resuscitate the young girl to ordinary life, but Christian readers may have been meant to see the request of the father "that she may be saved and live" (5:23) and the result that the girl "rose" (5:42) as a foreshadowing of Jesus' gift of eternal life.[41] The scene ends with another instance of Marcan secrecy (5:43).

In 6:1-6 (SUNDAY 14) Jesus returns to Nazareth, his native place; and this constitutes an inclusion with his dealings with "his own" from Nazareth at the beginning of the section (3:21,31-35). His teaching in the synagogue produces skepticism. The local people remember him as a carpenter and know his family, and so both his religious wisdom and his mighty works have no plausible origin. Jesus acknowledges that a prophet is without honor in his own region, "among his own relatives,"[42] and in his own house. Despite all the parables and the miracles we have seen in the intervening chapters, Jesus' ministry has not produced faith among those who should know him, and his power (which, as we have seen, is related to faith) is ineffective there.

SENDING OUT THE TWELVE; FEEDING 5,000; WALKING ON WATER; CONTROVERSY; FEEDING 4,000; (6:7–8:26; SUNDAYS 15–16, 22–23)

This section begins with sending out the Twelve and ends with their continued misunderstanding (8:21) and has as a major theme Jesus' failed attempt to bring these disciples to satisfactory faith—a failure that will lead to the second part of the Gospel where he proclaims that only by his own suffering and death can that be brought about. In the opening subsection

---

[41] Jesus' raisings from the dead (the daughter of Jairus; the son of the widow of Nain [Luke 7:11-17]); Lazarus) are miraculous resuscitations to ordinary life, similar to those done by the OT prophets Elijah and Elisha (1 Kings 17:17-24; 2 Kings 4:32-37). Jesus' resurrection to eternal life is of a higher order, anticipating God's raising of the dead in the last days.

[42] In the context this would seem to refer also to Jesus' mother; both Matt and Luke omit this phrase from their version of the scene, probably because they knew that Mary had conceived Jesus through the Holy Spirit and could scarcely be included among those who did not honor Jesus.

Chapter 3. Mark

49

(6:7-33) we encounter once more Marcan intercalation, for the sending out *(apostellein)* of the Twelve is narrated in 6:7- 13 (SUNDAY 15) and their return in 6:30-32 (SUNDAY 16), with an account of Herod's activity "sandwiched" between in 6:14-29 to occupy the intervening time. The disciples' mission to preach a change of mind, drive out demons, and cure the sick is an extension of Jesus' own mission; and he gives them the power to accomplish this. The austere conditions (no food, money, luggage) would make it clear any results were not effected by human means; and probably Marcan Christians had come to expect such austerity of missionaries. Between the beginning and the end of the mission, in a passage omitted by the Lectionary, we are told that King Herod (Antipas) has killed JBap, and now he is worried that Jesus might be JBap come back from the dead.[43] The fate of JBap is a warning of what the fate of Jesus is likely to be—and the fate of those sent to carry on his work.

The Lectionary omits the rest of chapter 6 (vv. 34–56), which includes the feeding of the 5,000 and the walking on the water. Rather, it is at this point, as explained in note 35 above, that for five Sundays (17–21) the Lectionary reads from John. On SUNDAY 22 Mark is resumed with selections from 7:1-23, a controversy over ritual purity. Despite all the miracles, what specifically bothers the Pharisees and scribes who come from Jerusalem is that some of Jesus' disciples do not observe ritual purity, a concept that 7:3-4 has to explain to the readers (suggesting strongly that they are not Jews). The controversy leads Jesus to condemn overly narrow interpretations as human tradition that disregards and even frustrates the real thrust of God's commandment for purity of heart. While the basic attitude toward the Law in 7:8,15 plausibly comes from Jesus, many schol-

---

[43] Apparently Mark 6:17 is not recording precise history: Herodias was the wife not of Philip but of another brother named Herod, and many doubt that a Herodian princess would dance in the manner described. This may well be a popular story—further dramatized in art, music, and drama under the heading of Salome's dance of the veils, whereas the biblical account mentions neither Salome nor veils.

Christ in the Gospels of the Ordinary Sundays

ars suggest that the application that has him declare all foods clean (7:19) represents an insight developed within the tradition that Mark espouses. The hard-fought struggles over kosher food attested in Acts and Paul would be difficult to explain if Jesus had settled the issue from the beginning. A sharp contrast to the hostility of the Jewish authorities is supplied by the faith of the Syrophoenician woman (7:24-30; omitted in the Lectionary)[44] when Jesus was in the Tyre area. (It is scarcely accidental that Mark places in sequence a controversy over food and the surprising faith of a Gentile who comes spontaneously to Jesus; they were the two major issues that divided early Christians.) If the woman's child is healed at a distance, the next miracle involving the deaf man (7:31-37; SUNDAY 23) describes an unusual amount of contact between Jesus and the afflicted, including putting his spittle on the tongue and using a transcribed Aramaic formula *Ephphatha*. Mark indicates that the people's enthusiasm about Jesus' power overrides his command to secrecy.

Even if in origin the feeding of the 4,000 (8:1-9) may have been a duplicate of the earlier feeding, it has a strong cumulative effect in Mark as another manifestation of Jesus' stupendous power. It is unfortunate that the Lectionary omits what follows in 8:11-26, for passages therein dramatize climactically the utter unlikelihood that Jesus will be accepted or understood. In particular the healing of the blind man in stages (8:22-26), peculiar to Mark, serves as a parabolic commentary on the situation of the disciples stemming from all that Jesus has done for them thus far. The man does not regain his sight immediately, for the first action by Jesus gives him only blurry vision. Only when Jesus acts a second time does the man see clearly. The next half of the Gospel will describe what Jesus must do to

---

[44] Some have been offended by Jesus' response in 7:27, which is not egalitarian since it places the Jews first (the children) and refers to Gentiles as dogs. Such scandal, however, may reflect a failure to accept Jesus as a 1st-century Jew. Paul too put Jews first (Romans 1:16), and 1 Peter 2:10 echoes the OT thesis that the Gentiles had no status as a people.

Chapter 3. Mark

make the disciples see clearly, namely, suffer, be put to death, and rise.

THREE PASSION PREDICTIONS; PETER'S CONFESSION; THE TRANSFIGURATION; JESUS' TEACHING (8:27–10:52; SUNDAYS 24–30)

Part Two of Mark begins with Peter's confession of Jesus (8:27-30; SUNDAY 24). Early in Part One of Mark we heard negative judgments about Jesus ("He is beside himself"; "He is possessed by Beelzebul"). Peter's confession comes amid more positive evaluations of him as JBap, Elijah, and one of the prophets. This spokesman of the disciples who has been with Jesus since 1:16 goes even further by proclaiming him as the Messiah, but Jesus responds with the same command to silence with which he modified the demons' identification of him as God's Son (3:11-12). The two titles are correct in themselves, but they have been uttered without including the necessary component of suffering. Jesus now commences to underline that component more clearly with the first of three predictions of his own passion (8:31). Peter rejects this portrait of the suffering Son of Man, and so Jesus categorizes his lack of understanding as worthy of Satan. Not only will Jesus have to suffer, but so too will those who would follow him (8:34-35).

The sequential Sunday Lectionary omits the rest of chapter 8 and 9:1-29, but the transfiguration (9:2-10) is read on the 2d Sunday of Lent in Year B. It offers another example of the inadequate faith of the disciples. At the beginning of Part One of Mark the identity of Jesus as God's Son was proclaimed during his baptism by a voice from heaven; but the disciples were not present at that time, and thus far in the public ministry no follower of Jesus has made a believing confession of that identity. Now at the beginning of Part Two, as the hitherto hidden glory of Jesus is made visible to three of his disciples, the heavenly voice re-identifies Jesus. The scene echoes the greatest OT theophany, for it takes place on a mountain amidst the presence of Moses and Elijah, who encountered God on Sinai (Horeb). The

Christ in the Gospels of the Ordinary Sundays

"after six days" of 9:2 seems to recall Exodus 24:16, where cloud covers Sinai for six days and only on the day after that does God call to Moses. Awkwardly Peter proposes to prolong the experience by building three tabernacles, even as the Tabernacle was built after the Sinai experience (Exodus 25–27; 36–38), but in reality he is terrified and does not know what to say (Mark 9:6). The discussion on the way down from the mountain brings up echoes from the passion prediction (namely, that the Son of Man must suffer and will rise from the dead), but now in relation to Elijah. The implicit identification of Elijah as JBap who came before Jesus and was put to death (9:13) may represent the result of early church reflection on how to relate the two great Gospel figures in the light of the OT.

The story of a boy with a demon (9:14-29; omitted by the Lectionary) whom Jesus' disciples are unable to expel because of inadequate faith is recounted by Mark at unusual length. The passage in Mark 9:30-48 (SUNDAYS 25–26) contains a mixture of material. It opens with Jesus' second prediction of the passion, which once again the disciples do not understand.[45] In Capernaum Jesus gives his disciples varied instructions pertinent to the kingdom—gathered here as an important last communication before Jesus arrives in Jerusalem to die. In 9:33-35 Jesus warns the Twelve not to seek to be greatest in the kingdom but a servant. The inclusiveness of the kingdom is exemplified in 9:36-41 by Jesus' command to receive a child (i.e., an insignificant person) in his name and his maxim "Whoever is not against us is for us." The protectiveness against scandal (i.e., causing to sin: 9:42-48) would be heard by Mark's readers as pertaining not only to his lifetime but to theirs.

The journey to Judea, instructing the crowds, and a question of the Pharisees are the context for Jesus' teaching on marriage and divorce (10:2-12; SUNDAY 27). The Pharisees on the basis of

---

[45] The difficulty in dismissing all these predictions as totally postJesus creations is exemplified in 9:31, where many scholars recognize Semitic features and old tradition.

Deuteronomy 24:1-4 would allow a husband to write out a note divorcing his wife because of "an indecency in her," and rabbis debated whether that indecency had to be something very serious or could be trivial. But Jesus, appealing to Genesis 1:27; 2:24 for the unity created by marriage, would forbid breaking the marriage bond, so that remarriage after a divorce constitutes adultery. (A similar attitude is found among the Jews who produced the Dead Sea scrolls.) A form of the prohibition is preserved in Matt (twice), Luke, and 1 Corinthians 7:10-11; and so it is not unlikely that historically there was a controversy in Jesus' life between him and other Jews who held different views about the issue. The difficulty of his position was recognized by early Christians, and the saying soon gathered comments. For instance, Mark 10:12, which extends the statement to a wife divorcing her husband (not a practice envisioned in OT law), is probably an adaptation to the situation of the Gentile hearers of the Gospel, where women could divorce men.[46] Jesus next returns to the issue of those who enter the kingdom (10:13-31). Most think that underlying the children passage in 10:13-16 there is a correction of a wrong attitude that would demand achievement, abilities, behavior, or status on the part of those who are brought to the kingdom, whereas for Jesus the kingdom/rule of God requires only human receptivity, of which the child is a good symbol. This interpretation brings Mark quite close to Paul's notion of justification by faith. But how do adults show or express receptivity? That is the issue behind the section 10:17-30 (SUNDAY 28), which begins with the question proposed by a rich man. In response Jesus does not depart from the commandments of God enunciated in the OT; but when the man

---

[46] Matt 19:9 has an exceptive phrase ("Whoever divorces his wife *except for immorality* [*porneia*] and marries another commits adultery [verb: *moichasthai*]," that also appeared in Matt 5:32, but in none of the other three forms of the divorce prohibition (Luke, Mark, 1 Corinthians). Although *porneia* can cover a wide range of immorality, a likely interpretation is a reference to marriages within what Jews regarded as forbidden degrees of kindred. Matt would be insisting that Jesus' prohibition of divorce did not apply to such marriages contracted by Gentiles who had come to believe in Christ.

Christ in the Gospels of the Ordinary Sundays

says he has observed them, Jesus lovingly asks him to sell his possessions and give the proceeds to the poor. Is that part of what is necessary to inherit eternal life, or does it apply only to a special discipleship of walking with Jesus? Certainly not all the early Christians sold their possessions; yet 10:24-27 shows that Jesus is demanding what is impossible by human standards but not by God's. Those who make great sacrifices for Jesus' sake will be rewarded both in this age and in the age to come (10:29-31); but the phrase "with persecutions," whether from Jesus or Mark, is an important realistic touch about their fate.

After Jesus' third and most detailed prediction of the passion (10:32-34), James and John raise the issue of the first places in the kingdom (10:35-45; SUNDAY 29). The challenge by Jesus to imitate him in drinking the cup and being baptized is symbolically a challenge to suffering. (The flight of the disciples at Gethsemane will show that their confident "We can" response is overly optimistic.) Although in the kingdom there are distinguished places prepared (by God), the disciples must learn that the Gentile pattern where kings lord it over people is not to be followed in the kingdom that Jesus proclaims. There service is what makes one great. "The Son of Man did not come to be served but to serve and to give his life as a ransom for many" (10:45) is a fitting summary of the spirit of this kingdom, a spirit anticipated in Isaiah 53:10-12.

The journey toward Jerusalem has a final scene in the Jericho area when Jesus heals the blind Bartimaeus (Mark 10:46-52; SUNDAY 30). This man who persists in crying out to Jesus for mercy when others tell him to be silent is symbolic of the many who will come to Christ and hear "Your faith has saved you." Mark offers us this scene of gaining sight as a positive element before the somber scenes he is about to describe in Jerusalem.

MINISTRY IN JERUSALEM: ENTRY; TEMPLE ENCOUNTERS; ESCHATOLOGICAL DISCOURSE (11:1–13:37; SUNDAYS 31–33)

The narrative gives the impression that everything described in these chapters takes place on three days (11:1,12,20). On the first

Chapter 3. Mark

day Jesus enters Jerusalem (11:1-10), a reading used for the procession with palms on Passion (Palm) Sunday in Year B. Two disciples are sent from Jesus' base of operations on the Mount of Olives, and all is as he foretold. He sits on the colt that they bring back (perhaps an implicit reference to Zechariah 9:9 about the coming of Jerusalem's king); and he is acclaimed by a hosanna cry of praise, by a verse from Psalm 118:26, and by the crowd's exclamation about the coming of the kingdom of "our father David." Thus Jesus is being proclaimed as a king who will restore the earthly Davidic realm—an honor but another misunderstanding.

The Sunday Lectionary skips over the actions of Jesus (cursing the fig tree, cleansing the Temple precincts) and the parables that are part of the controversies with the Jewish authorities in Jerusalem. By way of an exception to his hostile portrayal of those who interrogate Jesus, Mark describes a sensitive scribe who asks about the greatest commandment (12:28-34; SUNDAY 31) and wins Jesus' approbation as being not far from the kingdom of God. The opening line of Jesus' response is fascinating; for it cites the Jewish daily prayer, the Shema ("Hear, O Israel . . .") from Deuteronomy 6:4. This means that decades after Christian beginnings Gentiles were still being taught to pray a Jewish prayer as part of the fundamental demand placed by God! The two commandments inculcated by Jesus, combining Deuteronomy 6:5 and Leviticus 19:18, share a stress on love that became what Christians would like to think of as the identifying characteristic of their religion—a characteristic, alas, too often lacking. Jesus' denunciation of the public display of the scribes provides a background for an account of genuine religious behavior, the widow's giving her mite (12:38-44; SUNDAY 32).

Most of Jesus' activity in Jerusalem thus far has been in the Temple area; and it is after reflecting on the magnificent Temple buildings that, seated on the Mount of Olives, he delivers the Eschatological Discourse (13:1-37)—the last speech of his ministry that looks to the endtimes. The discourse is a collection of

Christ in the Gospels of the Ordinary Sundays

dire prophetic warnings (demolition of the Temple buildings; forthcoming persecution of the disciples; need to be watchful) and apocalyptic signs (deceivers, wars, desolating abomination standing where it should not be, phenomena in the sky). Interpretation presents many problems. Assuming that it is sequentially arranged and that Jesus had a detailed knowledge of the future, some have attempted to identify from our point of view what has already happened and what is yet to come. (Literalism particularly distorts the meaning if symbolic elements from OT and intertestamental apocalyptic writings are taken as exact descriptions of expected events.) Even those who appreciate the symbolic nature of apocalyptic and do not take a literalist approach think that in part the Marcan account is colored by what the evangelist knows to have already taken place, for example, persecution in synagogues and before governors and kings. For most readers the "bottom line" from reading through the discourse is that no precise timetable is given: On the one hand Jesus' followers are not to be misled by speculations and claims that the end is at hand; on the other hand they are to remain watchful. One portion of the discourse (13:24-32) is read on SUNDAY 33, and another (13:33-37) on the 1st Sunday of Advent in Year B (see note 27, above). Instead of a passage from Mark for SUNDAY 34 (the feast of Christ the King), the Lectionary once more shifts to John (18:33-37)—a section from the passion narrative where Jesus explains his kingship to Pilate.

* * *

Passages from the rest of Mark, which constitute the passion, burial, and resurrection narratives in chapters 14–16, are read in Passiontide (particularly Palm Sunday) of Year B and Eastertime. They have already been discussed in this Liturgical Press series of books in *A Crucified Christ in Holy Week* and *A Risen Christ in Eastertime.*

Chapter 3. Mark

Chapter 4

The Gospel according to Luke
(Liturgical Year C)

This is the longest of the four Gospels. Yet it is only half of the great Lucan written work, for Acts was originally joined to it as part of a two-volume tome that in length constitutes over one-quarter of the NT—a magnificent narrative that blends together the story of Jesus and that of the early church. Perhaps more than in any other Gospel the story is intrinsic to the theology; and part of that theology is the way the Gospel story of Jesus prepares for what happens in Acts, especially to Peter, Stephen, and Paul. Luke departs from Mark more than does Matt and theologically can be said to stand part way between Mark/Matt and John.

INTRODUCTORY OBSERVATIONS

Precisely because the Gospel is related to Acts, a word is necessary about the authorship and plan of Luke before we begin a reflection on the sequential text of the Gospel, which begins to be read in the third or C Lectionary Year on *the 3d Sunday of the Ordinary Time* with 4:14. This Gospel was probably written about AD 85, give or take five to ten years. By traditional attribution the author was Luke, a physician, the fellow worker and traveling companion of Paul. (Less well attested tradition would make him a Syrian from Antioch.) A considerable number of scholars challenge that attribution on the grounds that some of the (inexact) information about Paul in Acts and the theological outlook there cannot be reconciled with authorship by one who traveled with him and knew him well. Yet prestigious scholars of equal rank point out that the companion of Paul implied in the passages of Acts that use "we" was probably not with Paul before 50 or during the years from 51 to 58 and that he wrote almost two decades after Paul's letters (which

Christ in the Gospels of the Ordinary Sundays

may not have been known to him). Thus on the basis of Acts, authorship by Luke, companion of Paul, cannot be ruled out.

Nor does what one can detect from the contents of the Gospel about the author refute the possibility of authorship by Luke. One can observe that this author (for whom I retain the traditional name "Luke" without prejudicing the identification issue) was an educated Greek-speaker who knew the Jewish Scriptures in that language and who was not an eyewitness of Jesus' ministry. Luke preserves about 65 percent of Mark, which he has taken over in large blocks. Even more than Matt, Luke eliminates or modifies elements in Mark that he deems insufficiently respectful to Jesus, his family, and companions. He also draws on a collection of the sayings of the Lord (Q) as well as some other available traditions, oral or written.[47] A gifted storyteller with a truly artistic sense of balance, he is the best Greek stylist among the evangelists and has a sense of Greco-Roman culture. He is not precise on Palestinian geography or Jewish family customs, and so probably he was not by birth a Palestinian or a Jew. Yet his book knowledge of Judaism and the Greek OT suggests that he may have been a convert to Judaism before he became a Christian.

From the evidence of the second volume (Acts), the Gospel[48] was addressed to churches affected directly or indirectly by Paul's mission—churches consisting mostly of Gentile Christians (Acts 28:25-28). Serious proposals center on areas in Greece or Syria; but a diagnosis of Luke's intended readers may be more difficult than for any other Gospel. The fact that the Gospel begins in Jerusalem and Acts ends in Rome suggests a sweeping view of the destiny of Christianity, and so Luke

[47] Q constitutes about 20 percent of the Gospel. Special Lucan sources have supplied the infancy narrative material, hymns (*Magnificat*, etc.), parables (good Samaritan, prodigal son, Lazarus and the rich man, etc.), information about JBap, Herod Antipas, and other historical figures.

[48] The manuscripts of Luke show a remarkable number of significant differences among themselves, so that some have argued for two editions (especially of Acts) done in different parts of the church.

Chapter 4. Luke

would not have been displeased to learn that his Gospel was meaningful to far more than the local churches known to him.

The Prologue (1:1-4)[49] indicates that not apologetics against adversaries but assurance to fellow Christians was Luke's goal: "So that you may realize what certainty you have of the instruction you have received." Luke acknowledges dependence on eyewitness tradition and shows an awareness of other accounts of Jesus but stresses that this account will be orderly. Part of that orderliness is apparent in the way Luke dramatizes his theology in geography and salvation history. One example of geographical theology is that Jesus' whole life was spent in the confines of Judaism, and so the Gospel begins and closes in the Jerusalem Temple (1:8-11; 24:52-53). The church moves from the Jewish world to the Gentile world, and so Acts (1:4; 28:16) begins in Jerusalem and ends in Rome. Another geographical interest (visible in the Gospel outline on an accompanying page) is the prominence given to Jesus' "Journey to Jerusalem," an anticipation of the attention to be paid in Acts to the journeys of Paul. Such traveling is an enduring encouragement to Christians to proclaim Christ to the ends of the earth; and, indeed, in the course of time many great developments in theology have come as the Christian message has had to adapt itself to geographically new and different cultures.

Commentators have traced with many variations the orderly character of Luke's vision of salvation history. One workable proposal is that Luke envisioned three divisions: *Israel* (=a story recounted in the Law and the Prophets, or OT—see Luke 16:16); *Jesus* (=a story recounted in his Gospel, beginning in Luke 3:1); the *Church* (=a story recounted in Acts, beginning in 2:1 and continuing beyond to the ends of the earth until the Son of Man comes). Thus Jesus is the centerpiece binding together Israel

[49] Resembling the prefaces of Greek histories written to guide the reader, this is one long sentence in a style more formal than that found elsewhere in the Gospel. Among the four evangelists only Luke and John write a few verses explaining reflectively what they think they are about: John at the end (20:30-31), Luke at the beginning.

Christ in the Gospels of the Ordinary Sundays

Outline of the Gospel According to Luke

---

and the Church—he is the fulfillment of what has been written in the OT Scriptures (4:21); and when he ascends to heaven, the Spirit sent by the Father (Acts 1:4,8; 2:1-4) makes possible the spread of the Church. The time period associated with Jesus may be calculated from the baptism to the ascen-

Chapter 4. Luke

sion on Easter Sunday evening (Luke 24:50-51—see Acts 1:22). Respectively, transitional from the OT to Jesus and from Jesus to the Church are two bridges constructed by the evangelist. In Luke 1–2 OT characters representing Israel (Zechariah, Elizabeth, the shepherds, Simeon, Anna) come across the bridge to meet Gospel characters (Mary, Jesus); in Acts 1 the Jesus of the Gospel comes across the bridge to instruct the Twelve and prepare them for the coming Spirit who will establish the Church through their preaching and miracles. Thus there is continuity from the beginning of God's plan to the end.

GUIDANCE TO BEGINNING THE SEQUENTIAL USE OF LUKE IN THE LECTIONARY

On the 3d Sunday of the Ordinary Time in Year C the Lectionary begins the consecutive reading of Luke with 4:14. Let me introduce that with a few paragraphs calling attention to the evangelist's initial portrayal of Jesus. As with Matt, so also with Luke: The liturgy separates the infancy narrative (Luke 1–2) from the body of the Gospel and treats it in the last part of Advent and in the Christmas season (with the feast of the Presentation, February 2, included as a prolongation). I have discussed this material already in my previous books on Advent and Christmas in this Liturgical Press series (see table at the end of this book), and so I shall not repeat that discussion here. From those initial chapters of Luke readers should keep in mind the strong Jewish tone of the stories about JBap and Jesus. The hymns scattered throughout them (*Magnificat, Benedictus, Gloria in Excelsis, Nunc Dimittis*), which may be reminiscences of the earliest Christian prayers, are basically mosaics of OT passages. The parents of JBap were of a Jewish priestly family and totally obeyed all the commandments and ordinances of the Lord (1:6). Over and over again Luke reminds us that in all they did the parents of Jesus followed what was prescribed in the Law (2:21,22-23,39,42). If eventually Christian preachers had to turn from Jews to Gen-

Christ in the Gospels of the Ordinary Sundays

tiles (Acts 28:25-28), that is not because Jesus rejected the heritage of Israel.[50]

Luke's account of the public activity of JBap (3:1-20) is relatively long and has been read on the 2d and 3d Sundays of Advent in this Year C of the Lectionary. As might have been anticipated from the attention given to JBap in the infancy narrative, where his annunciation and birth were made parallel to that of Jesus, Luke resoundingly highlights the importance of JBap's public appearance (probably *ca.* AD 29) by synchronizing it with the reigns of the emperor, the governors, and the high priests, so that it becomes a world event. With the expression "the word of God came to John the son of Zechariah" (3:2) Luke assimilates JBap's call to that of an OT prophet (Isaiah 38:4; Jeremiah 1:2; etc.). Quotation of the Isaian prophecy (40:3-5) about the voice crying in the wilderness, which is connected to JBap in all four Gospels, is extended to include "all flesh shall see the salvation of God" as part of Luke's theological concern for the Gentiles. Particularly Lucan is JBap's social teaching in 3:10-14 with its emphasis on sharing goods, justice for the poor, and kind sensitivity. All this is similar to what the Lucan Jesus will emphasize in his ministry, a similarity that explains 3:18, where JBap is said already to be preaching the gospel.

The brief Lucan account of the baptism of Jesus (3:21-22), which was read in the Lectionary of Year C on the feast of the Baptism (1st SUNDAY, Ordinary Time), indicates that Jesus was praying at that crucial moment (the Lucan theme of prayer will also mark the end of the ministry: 23:46). In response the Holy Spirit descends in *bodily* form here at the beginning of the Gospel, even as it will come in visible form on the Twelve at Pentecost at the beginning of Acts (2:1-4). Next Luke stops to recount Jesus' genealogy (3:23-38) before Jesus begins his ministry, thus imitating Exodus 6:14-26, which recounts Moses'

---

[50] Similarly Acts 2:46; 3:1 show the first followers of Jesus following Jewish Temple prayer practice. See also Acts 24:14, where Paul says, "I worship the God of our ancestors, believing everything commanded by the Law or written in the Prophets."

Chapter 4. Luke

genealogy after his early beginnings and before he begins his ministry of leading the Israelites from Egypt.[51]

The account of the testing/temptations of Jesus (4:1-13), which the liturgy reads on the First Sunday of Lent in Year C, is introduced by the indication that Jesus was "full of the Spirit," a Lucan emphasis to prepare for the prominent role of the Spirit in Acts (e.g., 6:5; 7:55). The Lucan temptations, like the Matthean, correct a false understanding of Jesus' mission.[52] Particularly noteworthy is that unlike Mark and Matt, Luke has no angels come to minister to Jesus and specifies that the devil left him till an opportune time. At the beginning of the passion, Luke alone among the Synoptics will be specific about the presence of Satan, the power of darkness (22:3,31,53); and on the Mount of Olives when Jesus is tested again, an angel will come to strengthen him (22:43-44), thus connecting the two testings of Jesus.

JESUS BEGINS GALILEE MINISTRY IN NAZARETH; ACTIVITIES AT CAPERNAUM; CALLS DISCIPLES (4:14–5:16; SUNDAYS 3–5)[53]

The Lectionary for Year C begins consecutive reading of Luke with 4:14.[54] There, with his sense of theological geography, Luke

---

[51] While Matt's genealogy descended from Abraham to Jesus, Luke's genealogy mounts to Adam (since Jesus will be a savior of all humanity, beyond the physical descent of Israel) and even to God (3:38). Luke's genealogy is never read in the Lectionary.

[52] P. 22, above. The most obvious difference between Matt and Luke is the order of the last two temptations. Was the Q order the same as Luke's, so that Matt changed it to have the scene end on the mountain, matching the mountain motif of Matt 5:1; 28:16? Or was the Q order the same as Matt's, so that Luke changed it to have the scene end at the Jerusalem Temple where the Gospel ends in 24:52-53? Most judge Matt's order more original.

[53] I remind readers of the suggestion on p. 22, above, as to how one might use the individual sections of my book to accompany the Lectionary passages.

[54] Actually on this Sunday the Lectionary emphasizes that it is really starting the Gospel according to Luke by beginning with the Lucan Prologue, 1:1-4, and then follows immediately with 4:14. I have commented on the Prologue above.

Christ in the Gospels of the Ordinary Sundays

calls attention to Jesus' return to Galilee; he will terminate the Galilean ministry with Jesus' departure toward Jerusalem (9:51). In between Luke places most of the public ministry account that he takes over from Mark, on which he imposes his own order. To explain why Jesus of Nazareth spent most of his ministry in Capernaum, Luke commences with the rejection of Jesus at Nazareth (4:14-30; SUNDAYS 3–4), which is recounted considerably later in Mark 6:1-6 and Matt 13:54-58. Also, the Nazareth scene is much expanded beyond Mark's "on the Sabbath he began to teach in the synagogue," for Luke supplies the content of the teaching as Jesus comments on the scroll of the prophet Isaiah (the sole Gospel evidence that Jesus could read). The passage (Isaiah 61:1-2), which reflects the Jubilee-year amnesty for the oppressed, is used to portray Jesus as an anointed prophet and is programmatic of what Jesus' ministry will bring about. (Presumably it would have appealed strongly to those of Luke's addressees among the lower classes—those won over by the preaching of Paul and his disciples described in Acts.) The rejection of Jesus the prophet by those in his own native place echoes Mark; but there is no Lucan suggestion that those rejecting him included his own household or his relatives (cf. Mark 6:4).[55] Jesus' turning to outsiders is justified by prophetic parallels. The fury of the people against Jesus, even to the point of trying to kill him, goes far beyond the Marcan account and serves from the very beginning to prepare readers for his ultimate fate.

Luke recounts activities connected with Capernaum (4:31-44), which now becomes the operational center of Jesus' Galilean ministry. This section is not read on Sundays, but a few remarks about it are useful to understand the picture of Jesus that Luke is developing. The first of twenty-one Lucan miracles (deeds of power) is an exorcism—even though the devil has departed until a more opportune time, Jesus will struggle with many

---

[55] Anything derogatory to Jesus' mother would conflict with the picture the evangelist painted of her in the infancy narrative.

demons. The healing of Simon's mother-in-law (4:38-39) omits the presence of the four fishermen-disciples from Mark's account because in Luke Jesus has not yet called them (see below). Compared to Mark 1:39, which has Jesus going through the synagogues of all Galilee, Luke 4:44 localizes the synagogues in Judea. That may illustrate the vagueness of Luke's ideas of Palestinian geography, since in the next verse (5:1) Jesus is still in Galilee, at the Lake.[56]

The miraculous catch of fish and the call of the disciples (Luke 5:1-11; SUNDAY 5) illustrate ingenious Lucan (re)ordering. The call of the first disciples that Mark had placed before the four Capernaum episodes has been moved after them and, indeed, after a fishing miracle that only Luke among the Synoptics records. That Jesus has healed Simon's mother-in-law and effected a tremendous catch of fish[57] makes more intelligible why Simon and the others followed Jesus so readily as disciples. The call of a Simon who confesses himself an unworthy sinner is a dramatic presentation of vocation and prepares the way for a calling of Paul, who was also unworthy because he had persecuted Christians (Acts 9:1-2; Galatians 1:13-15). The theme of leaving "everything" to follow Jesus (Luke 5:11) illustrates Luke's stress on detachment from possessions.

REACTIONS TO JESUS: CONTROVERSIES WITH THE PHARISEES; CHOICE OF THE TWELVE AND PREACHING TO THE MULTITUDE ON THE PLAIN (5:17–6:49; SUNDAYS 6–8)

Drawing on Mark 2:1–3:6, Luke presents a series of five controversies (5:17–6:11), in all of which Pharisees play a role. The controversies involve a paralytic, the call of Levi, fasting, picking grain, and healing on the Sabbath. In them Pharisees criticize many aspects of Jesus' behavior: his claim to be able to forgive sins, his associates, his failure to have his disciples fast,

---

[56] Or does Luke's Judea simply mean "the country of the Jews"?

[57] Here we encounter Luke's occasional similarity to John, for the fishing miracle occurs in a postresurrectional setting in John 21:3-11.

Christ in the Gospels of the Ordinary Sundays

their picking grain, and his own healing on the Sabbath. Even though none of this material is used in the Sunday Lectionary, it is worth remembering as background when we read the next subsection, where Luke turns to the favorable reactions to Jesus by recounting the choice of the Twelve (6:12-16)[58] and especially the sermon to the multitude on the plain (6:17-49). That preaching, which is read on SUNDAYS 6–8, is the Lucan parallel to Matt's Sermon on the Mount (Matt 5–7).[59] Matt's sermon was directed to the Twelve; but although in Luke the Twelve are with Jesus, he has healed "all" among a great multitude on a plain, and so the sermon is directed to all disciples. Four Lucan beatitudes open the sermon, echoing the program for the ministry read aloud in the Nazareth synagogue. These beatitudes address those who are actually poor, hungry, mournful, and hated "now." The accompanying "woes," perhaps of Lucan creation and resembling the contrasts in the *Magnificat*, hint at the antagonisms engendered among the addressees by the affluent. The comparable condemnation in James 2:5-7; 5:1-6 might suggest that the reason for the violent dislike was the practice of injustice by the rich. Yet as we shall see in later chapters, at times but not consistently, Luke seems to regard the very possession of wealth (unless distributed to the poor) as corrupting one's relationship to God. Luke's ideal is the community of those believers who give their possessions to the common fund, as he describes in Acts 2:44-45; 4:32-37.

Without the proclamations "You have heard it said . . . but I say to you" that characterize Matt 5:17-48, Luke 6:27-36 enunciates Jesus' values. Although sometimes these are called "the ethics of the kingdom," that designation is far more appropriate for Matt, where "kingdom" occurs eight times in the course of the Sermon on the Mount, than for Luke, who mentions

[58] The Lucan list of the Twelve Apostles (see also the Eleven in Acts 1:13) seems to stem from a different tradition from that of Mark 3:16-19 and Matt 10:2-4 (see note 20, above).

[59] Luke's composition from his own material (L), Mark, and Q is only about 30 percent as long as Matt's.

Chapter 4. Luke

"kingdom" only once in the whole sermon (6:20). Thus there is less eschatological tone to the startling demands of the Lucan Jesus for his disciples to love those who hate and abuse them. If, as the author of Luke-Acts would have known, the preaching of Jesus blessing the poor and the hungry attracted many of the slaves and lower class in the Roman world, the challenge to bless those who curse you and pray for those who maltreat you would have been just as difficult for them as the blessing on the poor was for the rich. Many interpreters have commented on the impossibility of running a society in the world known to us on the principle of turning the other cheek or giving your shirt to someone who has robbed you of your coat, but that very impossibility tells us that the kingdom of God has not been realized in our world. So long as there are those like St. Francis of Assisi who try to live out the spirit of the Lucan sermon, the hope that the kingdom envisioned by Jesus can come is not lost. The passage on not judging is an extension of love. We are reminded that the demands are addressed to all who would hear (6:27,47) and that the demands are not met by those who do not bear good fruit (6:43-45) and simply say "Lord, Lord" (6:46).

MIRACLES AND PARABLES THAT ILLUSTRATE JESUS' POWER AND HELP TO REVEAL HIS IDENTITY; MISSION OF THE TWELVE (7:1–9:6; SUNDAYS 9–11)

The Lucan form of the healing of the centurion's servant in 7:1-10 (SUNDAY 9) has two deputations sent to Jesus rather than having the official himself come, and has a servant *(doulos)* cured rather than a boy/son; it may be secondary (compare Matt 8:5-13; John 4:46-54). The story contrasts a Gentile's faith-response to Jesus with the Jewish authorities' rejection of him. This is a Gentile who has loved the Jewish nation and built the synagogue and thus foreshadows Cornelius, the first Gentile to be converted in Acts (10:1-2). The next miracle, the raising of the son of the widow of Nain (Luke 7:11-17; SUNDAY 10), is uniquely Lucan. This awesome manifestation of power gains Jesus christological recognition (7:16 echoes the prophet and divine visita-

Christ in the Gospels of the Ordinary Sundays

tion motif of 1:76-78) but also shows his compassionate care for a mother deprived of her only son.

The material in 7:18-35, which concerns the relation of Jesus to JBap, is not read in the Sunday Lectionary. Actually, as in the other Gospels, it is crucial for understanding Jesus, since Jesus' reaction to the fate of JBap shaped his own ministry. Part of his bitterness toward the Pharisees and the lawyers was rooted in their rejection of JBap, whose goodness was apparent to all the people, even the tax collectors.

This constitutes background for the beautiful story in Luke 7:36-50 (SUNDAY 11), which, in the context of a meal at the table of Simon the Pharisee, involves a penitent sinful woman weeping over and anointing Jesus' feet. It may be composite, since it involves a parable comparing two debtors. Is the Lucan story the same as that of the anointing of Jesus' head by a woman at the house of Simon the leper in Mark 14:3-9 and Matt 26:6-13, and that of the anointing of Jesus' feet by Mary, the sister of Martha and Lazarus, in John 12:1-8?[60] There is also a debate as to whether Luke's sinful woman was forgiven because she loved much or whether she loved much because she had already been forgiven. Either meaning or both would fit Luke's stress on God's forgiveness in Christ and a loving response. After the story of this woman Luke describes the Galilean women followers of Jesus (8:1-3) who had been cured of evil spirits and diseases. Three of them are named: Mary Magdalene; Joanna, wife of Chuza, Herod's steward; and Susanna— the first two will reappear at the empty tomb (24:10). Interestingly the other Gospels name Galilean women exclusively in relation to the crucifixion and resurrection, so that only

[60] Many think that two stories, one of a penitent sinner who wept at Jesus' feet during the ministry and the other of a woman who anointed Jesus' head with costly perfume, have become confused in the tradition that came down to Luke and John. Others argue for one basic story. Hagiographic tradition and legend glued these three stories together and further confused the situation by identifying Mary, sister of Martha, with Mary Magdalene, whence all the art depicting Mary Magdalene as a penitent prostitute with her hair loosed.

Chapter 4. Luke

Luke tells us of their past and that they served *(diakonein)* the needs of Jesus and the Twelve out of their means—a picture of devoted women disciples. In part this support anticipates the picture of women in Acts, for example, Lydia at Philippi (16:15).

Rejoining the outline of Mark at its parable chapter (4:1-20), Luke 8:4-15 recounts the parable of the sower and the seed and its explanation, interrupted by the purpose of the parables.[61] There is also a sequence of four miracle stories (8:22-56): calming the storm at sea, healing the Gerasene demoniac, resuscitating Jairus' daughter, and healing the woman with a hemorrhage. Next Luke continues with the sending out of the Twelve (Luke 9:1-6). Having manifested his power, Jesus shares it with the Twelve by giving them authority over demons and sending them to preach the kingdom/gospel and to heal (9:2,6). Unfortunately none of the material from 8:1 to 9:6 is incorporated in the Sunday Lectionary.

QUESTIONS OF JESUS' IDENTITY: FEEDING OF THE 5,000, PETER'S CONFESSION, FIRST AND SECOND PASSION PREDICTION, TRANSFIGURATION (9:7-50; SUNDAY 12)
While the Twelve are away, we are told of Herod's having beheaded JBap (Luke 9:7-9).[62] The important point is the tetrarch's curiosity about Jesus (preparing for 13:31 and 23:8). The theme of Jesus' identity is followed out in the subsequent scenes. They begin with the return of the Twelve Apostles and the feeding of the 5,000 (9:11-17, read on the feast of Corpus Christi in Year C),

---

[61] The hundredfold yield of the seed that fell into good soil is interpreted as those who hear the word, hold it fast in an honest and good heart, and bring forth fruit with patience (8:15). This leads into the arrival of Jesus' mother and brothers (8:19-21). Although drawn from Mark 3:31-35, the import is entirely changed. There is no longer an unfavorable contrast between the natural family and a family of disciples; rather there is only praise of the mother and brothers as hearing the word of God and doing it—they exemplify the good seed and fit the criterion of discipleship.

[62] Luke's omission of the whole Marcan account of Herod's banquet and the dance of Herodias' daughter may reflect a distaste for the sensational.

Christ in the Gospels of the Ordinary Sundays

an adapted form of Mark 6:30-44. (For the theology of this multiplication of loaves, see p. 30, above.) Then in what is dubbed by scholars the "Big Omission," Luke skips over Mark 6:45–8:26, thereby leaving out everything from after the feeding of the 5,000 to after the feeding of the 4,000.[63]

Rejoining Mark's outline at Mark 8:27, Luke next presents the threefold proposal about who Jesus is and Peter's confession (9:18-20), introduced by the typical Lucan note that Jesus was praying. In the sequence Peter's "the Messiah of God" is Luke's way of answering Herod's "Who is this?" ten verses earlier. This confession is greeted by Jesus' first passion prediction (9:21-22), but there is in Luke (unlike Mark/Matt) no misunderstanding by Peter and no chastisement of him. The combined 9:18-24 is read on SUNDAY 12; after that, however, the sequential Lectionary skips Jesus' teaching about the cross (to be taken up "daily") in 9:23-27; the miracle story of the boy with a demon (9:37-43a), where typically Luke suppresses most of the Marcan emphasis on the incapacity of the disciples to heal this child; and the second prediction of the passion and the dispute about greatness (9:43b-50)—once more softening the picture of the disciples. The one passage from this whole area of Luke that makes its way into the Sunday Lectionary (on the 2d Sunday of Lent in Year C) is the transfiguration (9:28-36), set in the context of Jesus praying. The Lucan account describes glory as present already in Jesus' earthly career (9:32—an outlook present in John's Gospel also); yet it also affirms the suffering aspect of the Son of Man, for Jesus talks to Moses and Elijah about his "exodus," that is, his departure to God through death in Jerusalem. Both glory and suffering are affirmed by God's voice that identifies Jesus as Son and Chosen One (Suffering Servant).

* * *

[63] Presumably the Lucan evangelist saw these as doublets and decided to report only one; but the differences from the Marcan account of the 5,000 and the presence of another variant in John 6:1-15 may mean that Luke combined two accounts in the one multiplication of the loaves he reports.

Chapter 4. Luke

At this point Luke begins his long account of the journey to Jerusalem (9:51–19:27), which really constitutes the second half of the Gospel account of Jesus' public ministry. In 9:51 the evangelist introduces it by a subpreface (somewhat comparable to 3:1-2) to mark off major change. The time is coming for Jesus to be taken up (to heaven), and so he sets his face for Jerusalem, where he is to die. Luke is portraying a Jesus who knows his destiny and accepts it from God. The long journey is (an artificial) framework, as Luke leaves the Marcan outline for almost all this second half of the Gospel and inserts large blocks from Q and from his own sources. The choice of a journey as a framework is probably dictated by a desire to create a parallel to Paul's journeying in Acts. This section of the Gospel is most characteristically Lucan and supplies proportionately a high percentage of Sunday readings. The material may be divided into three subsections according to the points in 13:22 and 17:11, where Luke reminds us of the framework of the journey.

FIRST TO SECOND MENTION OF JERUSALEM (9:51–13:21; SUNDAYS 13–20)

We have seen some parallels between the Gospels of Luke and John, but now we perceive that they are also far apart. Among the Gospels only Luke has the hostile encounter with a Samaritan village (9:51-56; SUNDAY 13), which is diametrically the opposite of the warm reception given Jesus by the Samaritans in John 4:39-42. Very Lucan is Jesus' refusal of the vengeance upon the Samaritans proposed by James and John. The dialogue with three would-be followers (9:57-62) highlights the absolute demand imposed by the kingdom. We saw a sending of the Twelve in Mark 6:7-13, Matt 10:5-42 (woven into the Mission Discourse), and Luke 9:1-6. Only Luke has a second mission, the sending of the seventy-two (10:1-12; SUNDAY 14). The doubling may be designed to prepare for Acts, where the Twelve function prominently at the beginning of the mission only to have the initiative pass to others, like Paul, Barnabas, and Silas. The need for a second sending in the Gospel (10:2) is explained

Christ in the Gospels of the Ordinary Sundays

by the size of the harvest. Does the designated "seventy-two" echo for Luke the LXX numbering of the nations in Genesis 10:2-31 and thus prognosticate the ultimate extent of the harvest? Joy at the subjection of the demons marks the Lucan return of the seventy-two (10:17-20)—compare the unemotional return of the Twelve in 9:10. Jesus sums up their mission (and perhaps the mission of the church as Luke has known it) in terms of the fall of Satan.[64] Why the disciples should rejoice because their names are written in heaven (Luke 10:20) is explained by what follows (not read in the Sunday Lectionary). Jesus thanks the Father for revelation (10:21-22), a passage that has Johannine parallels. That the disciples have been chosen by the Son to receive the revelation is shown in the blessing of 10:23-24, a macarism that acknowledges what they have seen.

The reading for SUNDAY 15 begins with the lawyer's question about eternal life and Jesus' response about the love of God and neighbor (10:25-28). Although the lawyer is posing a test, Jesus likes his answer; and that leads into further probing by the lawyer and the parable of the good Samaritan (10:29-37), which is peculiar to Luke. Since the commandment to love leads to (eternal) life, the lawyer seeks casuistically to know to whom the commandment applies; but he is told that one can define only the subject of love, not the object. The Samaritan is a subject whose range of love is unlimited, perhaps preparing for Acts 8 with its positive picture of the reaction of Samaritans to the gospel. The story of Martha and Mary (10:38-42; SUNDAY 16) is another instance where material peculiar to Luke has Johannine parallels (John 11:1-44; 12:1-8). Yet there are also major differences: The brother, Lazarus, is absent from Luke; and the family's home at Bethany in John is two miles from Jerusalem, not a village on the way from Galilee and Samaria to Jerusalem, as in Luke. The import of the Lucan story is that heeding the word of Jesus is the only important thing—a lesson harmonious

[64] The authority over serpents and scorpions given to them in 10:19 is similar to that in the postresurrectional mission in the Appendix or Long Ending attached to Mark's Gospel (16:17-18).

Chapter 4. Luke

with the earlier answer about the love of God and neighbor as the basic observance necessary for eternal life. It demonstrates that what is required is not complicated.

Similarly uncomplicated is the instruction given to the inquiring disciple about the Lord's Prayer (11:1-4; SUNDAY 17)—a shorter and in some ways older wording than that preserved in Matt (p. 24, above) but also less eschatological. The encouragement to pray is continued by the uniquely Lucan parable of the insistent friend (11:5-8), a story redolent of Palestinian local color, for it envisions the whole family crowded into a single-room house. Q material on insistence in asking (11:9-13) is added to make the point. The most important variant from Matt 7:7-11 is the promise in Luke 11:13 to those who ask: Matt has good things given by the heavenly Father; Luke has the Holy Spirit given, as verified in Acts.

The Sunday Lectionary omits all the material from 11:14 to 12:12, a good deal of which describes controversies (and in the Gospel sequence prepares readers for the struggle to take place at Jerusalem in the passion).[65] One omission is a particular loss: the peculiarly Lucan beatitude cried out by the woman in the crowd (11:27-28). The interchange involves two blessings with priority being given to obedience to God's word—this priority has been anticipated in the two blessings of 1:42-45. SUNDAY 18 resumes sequential reading with the pericope on greed and the parable of the rich barn builder (12:13-21), which is distinctively Lucan. The hope to divide an inheritance equally or to enlarge a growing business, understandable in itself, runs against the contention that a consuming interest in material possessions is not reconcilable with interest in God. Ideally Christians are asked to live by the maxim "One's life does not depend on what one possesses" (12:15; see Acts 2:44; 4:34). The fate of the barn builder reflects the expectation of an individual judgment

---

[65] The assurance that "the Holy Spirit will teach you what you ought to say" when facing hostile synagogue and secular authorities (Luke 12:11-12) takes on added significance in stories that illustrate the trials of Christians in Acts.

Christ in the Gospels of the Ordinary Sundays

taking place before the general judgment at the end of the world.

The reading for SUNDAY 19 (12:32-48) begins with the instruction "Sell your possessions and give alms" (12:33), but then Luke shifts the topic to the necessity of faithful watchfulness. In the midst of Q material (that Matt 24:43-51 has incorporated into the Eschatological Sermon) Luke 12:41 is an insert: a question by Peter as to whether this teaching is "for us or for all," which is never specifically answered. However, since the next saying involves a steward who takes good care of the household, one may judge that there is a greater obligation on the apostles and on Christian leaders. The threat of punishment for the servant who does not watch in 12:46 is qualified by the Lucan addendum in 12:47-48 distinguishing between the punishment of those who had knowledge and those who did not. (In narrating the hostile treatment of Jesus in the passion, Luke will be the most attentive of all the Gospels to distinguish between the leaders and the people.) That distinction leads into a frightening description of the diverse results of Jesus' ministry (12:49-53; SUNDAY 20). In eschatological language Jesus speaks of the fire he is to bring on the earth and the baptism of being tested that is part of his destiny. Division, not peace, will be the result; the prediction in Luke 2:34 that Jesus was set for the fall and rise of many in Israel is now made more precise in terms of how families will be split. Since other statements esteem peace (2:14; 19:38) and unified families (role of JBap in 1:17), the results of Jesus' ministry are ambivalent, with a thrust in both directions. Evidently much of this will happen soon, for Jesus expresses ire at people's inability to read the signs of the present time (12:54-56).

In 13:1-9 (read in Year C on the 3d Sunday of Lent) Luke offers examples of destruction to inculcate repentance. We have no other knowledge of Galileans who were killed by Pilate while offering sacrifice (at Jerusalem) or of the fall of a tower in Siloam (a pool in Jerusalem), although some have thought that the former incident explains the enmity between Herod, the

Chapter 4. Luke

tetrarch of Galilee, and Pilate, which Luke reports in 23:12. The parable of the fig tree (13:6-9) offers one more chance for the tree's bearing fruit before being cut down. Many have wondered if it is not a benevolent Lucan form of the cursing of the fig tree in Mark 11:12-14,20-23 and Matt 21:18-21 and thus a miracle that has become a parable. The Lectionary omits 13:10-21, the healing of a crippled woman and the twin parables of the mustard seed and the leaven.

SECOND TO THIRD MENTION OF JERUSALEM (13:22–17:10; SUNDAYS 21–27)

As Jesus moves on to Jerusalem and passes through cities and towns (13:22-30; SUNDAY 21), a tone of pessimism appears. Evidently not many are listening, and so the question arises whether only a few are to be saved. Jesus' answer underlines the unpredictability of response: Some of those invited last will be first, and the first will be last. The Lectionary omits a key passage (13:31-33) for understanding Luke's sequence, since the Pharisees' report of Herod's homicidal hostility offers the explanation for Jesus' going on to Jerusalem. The reader is probably meant both to think that the Pharisees are telling the truth and to distrust their motives, since they may have been trying to get Jesus off the scene by urging him to save his life through departure from Galilee. Paradoxically, Jesus knows that going to Jerusalem will lead to his death. (Herod will reappear during the Roman trial when Pilate turns Jesus over to him for judgment.) Jesus' thoughts about his destiny leads into the plaintive apostrophe to Jerusalem (13:34-35): As a prophet Jesus will die there, but the city will be punished for what it does to prophets.

The next three episodes (14:1-24) are set in the home of a prominent Pharisee: the Sabbath cure of a man with dropsy, two instructions about conduct at dinner, and the parable of the great banquet. The middle one, read on SUNDAY 22, offers an interesting contrast. Sitting in a lower place so that eventually, to everyone's admiration, you may be brought higher is both good

Christ in the Gospels of the Ordinary Sundays

manners and self-serving. But inviting to a banquet beggars and the infirm and not inviting one's friends and relatives represents the upside-down eschatological values of the kingdom. Thus this teaching, peculiar to Luke, combines worldly and unworldly wisdom for those who live in a world where God's kingdom is coming near but has not fully come. Afterwards, without mentioning Jesus' departure from the Pharisee's home, Luke has Jesus talking to the accompanying multitude about the cost of discipleship (14:25-35; SUNDAY 23). Peculiarly Lucan are the prudential parables worthy of an OT Wisdom teacher about the need to calculate the cost before starting a house or beginning a war. This message is very different from the more prophetic stance of not worrying about the needs of this life, inculcated earlier in 12:22-34.

The whole next chapter consists of three parables: lost sheep, lost coin, lost (prodigal) son (15:1-32; SUNDAY 24; also 4th Sunday of Lent in Year C). Matt 18:12-14 works the lost sheep parable into the Sermon on the Church addressed to the disciples; Luke addresses it (and his own other two parables) to the Pharisees and scribes who object to Jesus' keeping company with sinners. The references to joy in heaven show that the parables give a lesson in God's loving mercy and dramatize the value of those whom others despise as lost. In the first two Luke has a man and woman respectively as dramatis personae (shepherd, housekeeper). The lost or prodigal son stresses that the elder brother should not be jealous of the father's benevolent treatment of the sinful younger brother, and that fits the context of correcting the Pharisees' attitude toward sinners. Beyond that, the point made in the middle of the parable at 15:20 is important for understanding the concept of Christian love. The portrayal of the father running to the younger son and kissing him before he can give the prepared speech of repentance could serve as an illustration of Romans 5:8: "God's love for us is shown in that, while we were yet sinners, Christ died for us," and 1 John 4:10: "In this is love, not that we loved God but that God loved us."

Chapter 4. Luke

Many have found difficulty with the uniquely Lucan parable of the unjust steward (16:1-13; SUNDAY 25) because it seems to commend to the disciples a shady business practice; but what is praised is the prudent energetic initiative of the steward, not his dishonesty. Diverse sayings dealing with wealth have been attached to the parable, but it is debated at which verse they begin: 8b, 9, or 10. Overall they serve Luke's theological tenet that abundant money corrupts and that the right way to use it is to give it away to the poor and thus make friends who can help in heaven. The next Lectionary reading (16:19-31; SUNDAY 26), the uniquely Lucan parable of the rich man and Lazarus,[66] also concerns the damning effects of wealth. The different fates after death are not based on the rich man having lived a life of vice and Lazarus having been very virtuous; they are based on the rich man having had a comfortable and well-fed life, while Lazarus was hungry and miserable (16:25). This attack on the Pharisees' love for money (which would also serve as a warning for Christians, e.g., Acts 5:1-11) is made sharper by a second point, made at the end of the parable. If they do not listen to Moses and the prophets, they will not listen to someone come back from the dead. To Luke's readers/hearers this would appear prophetic, for Acts will show that people did not listen even after Jesus came back from the dead.

The topic changes as Jesus addresses to his disciples four unrelated warnings on behavior (17:1-10). Cautioning against scandalizing others, they stress forgiving fellow disciples, the power of faith, and the distinction between great achievement and duty. The last two on faith and duty are read on SUNDAY 27. The warning about doing one's duty, which is peculiarly Lucan, is an interesting challenge: The disciples who have followed Jesus might get the idea that they had done something great, but they are to tell themselves that they are unprofitable servants who have done only what they were supposed to do.

[66] This is another similarity between Luke and John: Only they mention a Lazarus, and the theme of resurrection from the dead is connected with him in both Gospels.

Christ in the Gospels of the Ordinary Sundays

This begins with the uniquely Lucan cleansing of the ten lepers, including the thankful Samaritan (17:11-19; SUNDAY 28). Jesus has been traveling toward Jerusalem since 9:51, and in 9:52 his messengers entered a Samaritan village. That at this point in the story he is still passing between Samaria and Galilee tells us that the journey is an artificial framework (and also that Luke may not have had a clear idea of Palestinian geography). Yet the framework explains why there is a Samaritan among the lepers, indeed, the sole leper to show gratitude and thus to receive salvation. His reaction anticipates the glad reception of the good news about Jesus by Samaritans in Acts 8:1-25. The Lectionary skips the eschatological teaching in 17:20-37 and picks up again with the uniquely Lucan parable of the unjust judge (18:1-8; SUNDAY 29), designed to encourage the disciples after the warnings of future judgment. If continued petitioning persuades a totally amoral judge, how much more will their persistent, confident prayer be heard by God, who vindicates the chosen ones. The theme of prayer leads into the Lucan parable of the Pharisee and the publican (or tax collector: 18:9-14; SUNDAY 30). Beyond exhibiting God's mercy to sinners, the story raises the issue of the rejection of the Pharisee, who is not justified. The Pharisee is not a hypocrite, for although a bit boastful, he has lived faithful to God's commandments as he understood them. Is the problem that although he thanks God, he has not shown any need of God or of grace or forgiveness? Or does the Lucan Jesus come close to Pauline thought that observing commanded works does not justify by itself?

The rest of the material in chapter 18 (15-43), including the third prediction of the passion,[67] is omitted in the Sunday Lectionary, which resumes with the colorful scene, set in Jericho

[67] Luke 18:31-34 hews close to Mark 10:33-34 even to the point of predicting that the Gentiles will spit upon and scourge the Son of Man—something that never happens in the Lucan passion narrative!

Chapter 4. Luke

and peculiar to Luke, involving Zacchaeus (19:1-10; SUNDAY 31). Beyond Jesus' kindness to a tax collector deemed a sinner, the story illustrates Luke's attitude toward wealth: Zacchaeus is a rich man, but salvation can come to his house because he gives half his goods to the poor.[68] The parable of the pounds (19:11-27), seemingly the Lucan variant of the Matthean parable of the talents (25:14-30), is not read, even though it has incorporated the distinctive story of a nobleman who goes to a far country to receive a kingship: His citizens hated him and sent an embassy to try to prevent his being appointed king, only to have him come back as king and slay them. This omission is unfortunate, for Luke means the story to prepare his readers for the rejection of Jesus in Jerusalem, his crucifixion as King of the Jews, his return in resurrection, and the ultimate destruction of Jerusalem.

ENTRY INTO JERUSALEM; ACTIVITIES IN THE TEMPLE AREA; ESCHATOLOGICAL DISCOURSE (19:28–21:38; SUNDAYS 32–33)

At the end of his long journey that began in 9:51 Jesus arrives at Jerusalem where his "exodus" or departure to God will take place. He will stay overnight at Bethphage and Bethany in the near environs of Jerusalem, but most of his activity there will be centered in the Temple area, and at the end he will deliver an eschatological discourse.

The royal entry into Jerusalem (19:28-40), read as part of the procession with palms on Passion (Palm) Sunday in Year C, stays close to the Marcan account (11:1-10) but changes the theme from the bystanders' enthusiasm for the arrival of the kingdom to the *disciples'* praise of Jesus as king (see John 12:13). In Luke 7:18-19 the disciples of JBap posed to Jesus their master's question, "Are you the one to come?" Now the disciples of Jesus confirm that he is. Luke includes a refrain about peace and glory that resembles the *Gloria in Excelsis* (2:14). The Lec-

---

[68] In 18:22-23 Jesus will ask a very wealthy would-be follower to give away *all* that he has to the poor. Is the spirit of sacrifice rather than the percentage the important issue?

Christ in the Gospels of the Ordinary Sundays

tionary skips the whole section in 19:41–20:26, which involves predictions of the destruction of Jerusalem,[69] the cleansing of the Temple, and the warning parable about the vineyard. There Luke describes how the chief priests and the scribes seek to destroy Jesus for this teaching but are frustrated by his popularity among "all the people"—a preparation for the benevolent Lucan picture of the people in the passion narrative.

The Lectionary picks up again with 20:27-38 (SUNDAY 32) with the hostile question posed by the Sadducees about the resurrection, a passage that not only highlights Jesus' stance about resurrection in general but also prepares us for his own resurrection. Once again the Lectionary passes over more of the Jerusalem disputes and teaching (20:39–21:4), so that when it resumes (21:5-19; SUNDAY 33) we are in the Eschatological Discourse. As in Mark/Matt, admiration of the Temple buildings elicits from Jesus a prediction of the destruction of the Temple (21:5-6); and that leads into a discourse on the last things—a speech particularly complicated in Luke by the fact that Jesus has already exhorted to eschatological vigilance in 12:35-48 and given eschatological teaching in 17:20-37. Unlike Mark/Matt, Luke situates the discourse in the Temple as a continuation of his daily teaching there (19:47; 20:1; 21:38); and there is more interest in what happens to Jerusalem, for some scholars would maintain that 21:8-24 refers to the fate of Jerusalem, while 21:25-36[70] refers to the fate of the world when the Son of Man comes. These points are worth noting: 21:12 speaks of persecution for the sake of Jesus' "name" (see Acts 3:6,16; 4:10; etc.); 21:13-15 promises that a wisdom that cannot be contradicted will be given when it is time to bear testimony (see 7:35; 11:49; Acts

[69] Scholars debate whether the description in 19:43 is so precise that Luke must have written or at least rephrased it after the historical destruction by the Romans. Also in place of Mark's abomination of desolation, Luke 21:20 speaks of Jerusalem surrounded by armies (from a knowledge of what happened in AD 70?).

[70] Passages from this (21:25-28,34-36) are read on the First Sunday of Advent in Year C. See note 27, above.

Chapter 4. Luke

6:3,10); 21:18 supplies extra confidence to Jesus' followers, for not a hair of their head will perish (see 12:7). The reading for SUNDAY 34 (feast of Christ the King) is taken from the Lucan passion narrative (23:35-43), as Jesus on the cross speaks to the "good thief"—see the next paragraph.

* * *

Passages from the rest of Luke, which constitute the passion, burial, and resurrection narratives in chapters 22–24, are read in Passiontide (particularly Palm Sunday) of Year C and Easter-time. They have already been discussed in this Liturgical Press series of books in *A Crucified Christ in Holy Week* and *A Risen Christ in Eastertime.*

Christ in the Gospels of the Ordinary Sundays

Chapter 5

The Gospel according to John
(Latter part of Lent; postEaster Season)

While all four evangelists had a theological goal, in a special
way the author of this Gospel has been known as John "the
theologian";[71] and many regard this as *the* theological masterpiece among the Gospels. Yet it has no liturgical year of its own
in the Lectionary. The fact that the principal consecutive reading
starts in the middle of Lent every year means that a special effort has to be made to call attention to the uniqueness of this
Gospel and why it has this unusual treatment in the Lectionary.
The following observations are made with that in mind.

INTRODUCTORY OBSERVATIONS

The Fourth and last of the canonical Gospels was written in the
period AD 80–110. More precisely, many think that the Gospel
was composed in two stages and date the writing of the body of
the Gospel by the evangelist to the 90s and the addition of further material by a final editor or redactor *ca.* 100–110 (about the
same time as the Third Epistle of John). Second-century tradition identified the evangelist as John the disciple, who reclined
on Jesus' bosom at the Last Supper—and this John was understood to be the son of Zebedee, one of the Twelve, who wrote
the Gospel in his old age as an improvement to supplement the
other Gospels. There are many internal reasons, however, to
doubt that the evangelist was an eyewitness apostle (apostles
are never mentioned!), and certainly this Gospel is no mere supplement.[72] Although I shall continue to use the traditional

---

[71] From the ancient Greek designation of him as *ho theologos*, traditionally
rendered in English as John "the divine," a usage stemming from that generous
time when theologians were known as divines.

[72] In fact, although it begins with JBap and ends with the passion/resurrection,
with the exception of the multiplication of the loaves and walking on the water,

designation (as I did for the other Gospels) by referring to the evangelist as "John," most commentators, Protestant and Catholic, do not think John son of Zebedee wrote the Gospel. Many think that the evangelist read the Synoptic Gospels or at least Mark, but a somewhat larger group thinks the Fourth Gospel reflects tradition independent of but similar to that preserved in Mark.

The compositional history is complicated by the Gospel's references (direct or indirect) in the Last Supper, passion, and resurrection accounts to a "disciple whom Jesus loved," a figure who is somehow involved in the composition (19:35; 21:24). He is never named; but besides the ancient thesis that he was John son of Zebedee, there are many modern theories about his identity. Probably the quest is misplaced energy, for his effectiveness as a model disciple is enhanced by the anonymity with which the Gospel surrounds him. Indeed, if we learned his name, we might be none the wiser; for he may not have been named in the rest of the NT.

Reading this very different Gospel is helped if we understand its origins. The following workable hypothesis, which with variations has considerable following, does justice to many factors visible in the final Gospel. In Stage One of Gospel Formation (Chapter 1, above) there was a disciple of Jesus, perhaps from the Jerusalem area, who had a different background from the other disciples who became known as the Twelve Apostles. His memories of the ministry and his interpretation of them had a different cast and history from those associated with preaching by the Twelve (Stage Two of Gospel Formation—their preaching became the common heritage in the larger church and was eventually digested by Mark). The Christian community in which this disciple lived and whose thought about Jesus he shaped made other converts of a different background, for example, Samaritans (see 4:39-42; 8:48). Their presence, plus the

---

John and the Synoptic Gospels have very different content for both the public ministry of Jesus and the Last Supper.

Christ in the Gospels of the Ordinary Sundays

very "high" christological articulation of the faith of the Johannine Christians (John is the only Gospel to call Jesus "God"), antagonized Jewish synagogue leaders, who thought the Johannine Christians no longer believed in one God but two. (Their hostile charges about making Jesus equal to God are reflected in 5:18; 10:33; 19:7.) Hearings, trials, and debates shaped the Johannine tradition and explain the Gospel's strong emphasis on testimony, witness, and listing of arguments (see 5:31-47). Eventually the Johannine Christians were thrown out of the local synagogues (9:22,34; 12:42; 16:2), with the effect that (even though many of them were of Jewish birth) they turned extremely hostile to "the Jews." They became all the more insistent that the correct evaluation of Jesus as divine decided one's relation to God—even to the point of becoming corrective of others who claimed to follow Jesus (6:60-66; 12:42-43). More than likely the disciple lived through many of these developments and served as guide and encouragement, especially when the Johannine Christians were orphaned by the synagogues. That made him the model disciple for the community, the one who embodied what the love of Jesus meant. In short, to the community he was par excellence "the disciple whom Jesus loved," the Beloved Disciple.

All this (reconstructed) community history preceded the writing of the Fourth Gospel (thus before Stage Three of Gospel Formation); and although the evangelist would have been influenced by it, he was not writing about the past or trying to persuade or refute adversaries. Probably a disciple of the Beloved Disciple,[73] the evangelist reorganized the tradition he received[74]

[73] Plausibly there was a number of Johannine writing disciples, that is, a "school" or following influenced by the Beloved Disciple; see 21:24: "We know that his testimony is true"—the testimony of the Beloved Disciple who bears witness to these things. The school could have included the evangelist, the redactor or final editor of the Gospel, and the author(s) of the epistles.

[74] Some think the tradition consisted of sources (collection of "signs"; collection of discourses; passion narrative) that the evangelist combined; others think of a process of several editions in which combinations had already begun. In

Chapter 5. John

so that those who follow Jesus might have the kind of faith that would give them eternal life, namely, *the faith that Jesus was God's only Son possessing God's own life and had come into the world from above that people might be given that life (and thus be begotten by God) and become God's children*. To this reorganization the evangelist brought noteworthy dramatic skill, so that the Gospel's lengthy narratives, like those of the Samaritan woman (John 4), the man born blind (John 9), and Lazarus (John 11), became highly effective vehicles of encounters leading to faith. Apparently, after the basic Gospel was completed, a redactor made additions (chapter 21; perhaps 1:1-18), a process that took place early enough so that no text of the Gospel has been preserved without these "additions."[75] Although the Johannine tradition was shaped in the area of Palestine, the actual writing of the body of the Gospel probably took place elsewhere (traditionally and plausibly in the Ephesus area, but some opt for Syria).

GUIDANCE TO BEGINNING THE SEQUENTIAL USE OF JOHN IN THE LECTIONARY

On an accompanying page I give a brief outline of the Gospel that calls attention to the main themes of its theology as worked out in the flow of the narrative. There is no Sunday liturgical year of John, and the Lectionary usage every year is somewhat nomadic:[76] incipiently at Christmastime, partly in Lent, and

either case there is little to support the radical thesis that much of the material the evangelist included came from alien sources and had little to do with Jesus as he actually was.

[75] The story of the woman caught in adultery (7:53–8:11) is not part of the redaction. Found only in some manuscripts, it was probably an old story about Jesus added later to the Gospel by a copyist in an area where the church was overcoming its reluctance to forgive adultery. Gradually it found its way into manuscript copies, particularly in the West, and was accepted as canonical Scripture.

[76] One of God's graces in this more ecumenical period is that several different churches use the same Sunday Lectionary. A very perceptive discussion by a Lutheran scholar (on which I draw freely) is applicable to both the Lutheran

Christ in the Gospels of the Ordinary Sundays

Outline of the Gospel according to John

1:1-18   **Prologue**: An introduction to and summary of the career of the incarnate Word.

1:19–12:50   **Part One: The Book of Signs**: The Word reveals himself to the world and to his own, but they do not accept him:

1. Initial days of the revelation of Jesus to his disciples under different titles (1:19–2:11);

2. First to second Cana miracle; themes of replacement and of reactions to Jesus (chapters 2–4);

3. Old Testament feasts and their replacement; themes of life and light (chapters 5–10): Sabbath—Jesus, the new Moses, replaces the Sabbath ordinance to rest (John 5); Passover (6); Tabernacles (7:1–10:21); Dedication (10:22-42);

4. The raising of Lazarus and its aftermath; the coming of the hour (chapters 11–12).

13:1–20:31   **Part Two: The Book of Glory**: To those who accept him, the Word shows his glory by returning to the Father in death, resurrection, and ascension. Fully glorified, he communicates the Spirit of life:

1. The Last Supper and Jesus' Last Discourse (chapters 13–17);

2. Jesus' passion and death (chapters 18–19);

3. The resurrection: four scenes in Jerusalem (chapter 20); Gospel Conclusion (20:30-31): statement of purpose for this writing.

21:1–25   **Epilogue**: Galilean resurrection appearances; second conclusion.

and Roman Catholic Lectionaries: C. R. Koester, "The Fourth Gospel in a Three-Year Lectionary," *Word & World* 10 (no.1, 1990) 21–26.

Chapter 5. John

partly in the Eastertime. Consequently readers need to keep an eye on the Gospel's outline to get some sense of how the liturgical selection relates to the evangelist's intent. One can debate the wisdom of the framers of the Lectionary: Would introducing a fourth year into the Sunday cycle give greater attention to John and enable it to be read on its own terms? Or is the use of John every year a way of demonstrating that it is different from the particular Synoptic Gospel being read that year and that its exalted message needs to be heard always if we want a larger Gospel picture of Jesus? In one way John is timeless: Its eloquent statements about light, love, faith, and judgment can be effective by themselves without historical context. In another way John is timely, formulated in the context of a community's spiritual growth and reactions to its own era. For example, on the Fourth Sunday of the Easter period in each year of the triennial cycle, a different paragraph from John 10 (which portrays the Good Shepherd) is read, thus preserving an ancient tradition of a Good Shepherd Sunday from the pre-Vatican II liturgy. The picture of Jesus as the Good Shepherd who knows his sheep by name, loves them, and lays down his life for them is timeless. Yet the polemic against others who are thieves and bandits and hired hands who run away leaving the sheep to be scattered, while it is adaptable, probably was aimed by the evangelist at specific late-1st-century targets in the synagogues and other Christian groups. These targets are detectable when the chapter is read in its Gospel sequence.[77] To do justice to all the potentialities of such Gospel readings one needs to reflect not only on the pastoral concern of Christ for his sheep but also on the ways that his concern is helped and hindered by human pastoral care and church structure.

By way of another example, Jesus' magnificent Last Discourse (13:31–17:26) was spoken in the Gospel sequence on the

[77] For example, the Pharisees who refused to see, criticized in the immediately preceding 9:40-41.

Christ in the Gospels of the Ordinary Sundays

night before he died; but readings from it appear in the Lectionary on the Sundays and weekdays after Easter and before Pentecost.[78] Jesus spoke words like "I shall not leave you orphans: I am coming back to you; in just a little while the world will not see me any more, but you will see me because I have life and you will have life" (14:18-19). At the Last Supper their primary reference was to Jesus' return after his death, but in the liturgy they are shifted to an indefinite future coming. One should not ask which perspective is true, for his words have both a timely and a timeless aspect. It is not accidental that the evangelist has been portrayed as an eagle who by climbing on high can see what is to come before it arrives.

STYLISTIC FEATURES

John is a Gospel where style and theology are intimately wedded; and whether reading it or explaining it to others, one should be conscious of the features explained below.

1. *Poetic format.* In a few sections of John many scholars recognize a formal poetic style, even marked by strophes, for example, the Prologue and perhaps John 17. But the issue we need to consider is much wider: a uniquely solemn pattern, often dubbed semipoetic, in the Johannine discourses. The characteristic feature of this poetry would not be parallelism of lines (as in the OT) or rhyme, but rhythm, that is, lines of approximately the same length, each constituting a clause. Whether or not one agrees that the discourses should be printed in poetic format (as many Bibles do), the fact that Jesus speaks more solemnly in John than in the Synoptics is obvious. One explanation draws on the OT: There divine speech (by God through the prophets or by personified divine Wisdom) is poetic, signaling a difference from more prosaic human communication. The Johannine Jesus comes from God, and therefore it is appropriate that his words be more solemn and sacral.

---

[78] As the table at the end of this volume indicates, this material was already treated in my *Once and Coming Spirit at Pentecost.*

Chapter 5. John

2. *Misunderstanding*. Although he comes from above and speaks of what is "true" or "real" (i.e., heavenly reality), the Word-become-flesh must use language from below to convey his message. To deal with this anomaly, he frequently employs figurative language or metaphors to describe himself or to present his message.[79] In an ensuing dialogue the questioner will misunderstand the figure or metaphor and take only a material meaning. This allows Jesus to explain his thought more thoroughly and thereby to unfold his doctrine. Stemming from the Johannine theology of the incarnation, such misunderstanding has become a studied literary technique. Jesus is a stranger from above who will inevitably be misunderstood by humans from below. He speaks of heavenly realities using the language of this world, but people will think he is speaking of worldly things (which for them are the only realities).[80]

3. *Twofold meanings*. Sometimes playing into misunderstanding, sometimes simply showing the multifaceted aspect of revelation, often a double meaning can be found in a dialogue involving Jesus. *(a)* There are plays on various meanings of a given word that Jesus uses, meanings based on either Hebrew or Greek; sometimes the dialogue partner may take one meaning, while Jesus intends the other.[81] *(b)* In the Fourth Gospel the author frequently intends the reader to see several layers of meaning in the same narrative or in the same metaphor. This is understandable if we think back to the circumstances in which the Gospel was composed, involving several time levels: There is a meaning appropriate to the historical context in the public

---

[79] In a sense the Johannine figures or metaphors (16:29) are equivalent to the Synoptic parables, for in John the reality represented by the Synoptic kingdom of heaven stands among people in the person of Jesus. In the Synoptics the parables are frequently misunderstood, just as the metaphors are in John.

[80] See John 2:19-21; 3:3-4; 4:10-11; 6:26-27; 8:33-35; 11:11-13.

[81] For example, various terms in 3:3,8 (birth/begetting; again/from above; wind/Spirit); "lifted up" in 3:14; 8:28; 12:34 (crucifixion and ascension in return to God); "living water" in 4:10 (flowing water and life-giving water); "die for" in 11:50-52 (instead or on behalf of).

Christ in the Gospels of the Ordinary Sundays

ministry of Jesus; yet there may be a second meaning reflecting the situation of the believing Christian community. For example, the prediction of Jesus that the Temple sanctuary would be destroyed and replaced in 2:19-22 is reinterpreted to refer to the crucifixion and resurrection of Jesus' body. The Bread of Life Discourse seems to refer primarily to divine revelation and wisdom in 6:35-51a and to the Eucharist in 6:51b-58. As many as three different meanings may have been intended in the imagery of the Lamb of God (1:29,36: apocalyptic Lamb, paschal Lamb, and Suffering Servant who went to slaughter like a lamb).

4. *Irony.* A particular combination of twofold meaning and misunderstanding is found when the opponents of Jesus make statements about him that are derogatory, sarcastic, incredulous, or at least inadequate in the sense that they intend. However, by way of irony these statements are often true or more meaningful in a sense that the speakers do not realize but that the reader is supposed to recognize. For instance, when the Samaritan woman asks sarcastically, "Surely, you don't pretend to be greater than our ancestor Jacob who gave us this well?" (4:12), Jesus does not answer or need to—readers/hearers know that he is greater. When the Galilean Jews who know Jesus' father and mother pose an absurdity, "How can he claim to have come down from heaven?" (6:42), Jesus does not need to answer—readers/hearers know that the parentage that truly matters is his Father in heaven, about which these scoffers are ignorant.[82]

5. *Inclusions and transitions.* The careful structure of the Gospel is indicated by certain techniques. "Inclusion" means that John mentions a detail (or makes an allusion) at the end of a section that matches a similar detail at the beginning of the section. This is a way of packaging sections by tying together the beginning and the end. A large inclusion is illustrated by 1:1 ("The Word was God") and 20:28 ("My Lord and my

---

[82] See also 3:2; 7:35; 9:40-41; 11:50.

God").[83] By way of transition from one subdivision of the Gospel to the next, the evangelist likes to use a "swing" ("hinge") motif or section—one that concludes what has gone before and introduces what follows. For example, the Cana miracle terminates the call of the disciples in John 1, fulfilling the promise in 1:50 that the disciple who was called would see far greater things, but also opens the next subdivision of 2:1–4:54, which runs from the first Cana miracle to the second. The second Cana miracle concludes that subdivision but by stressing Jesus' power to give life (4:50) prepares for the next subdivision (5:1–10:42), where Jesus' authority over life will be challenged. Since the liturgy does not follow sequentially through John, an effort will be necessary to highlight what the evangelist intended.

6. *Parentheses or footnotes.* Frequently John supplies parenthetical notes, explaining the meaning of Semitic terms or names (e.g., "Messiah," "Cephas," "Siloam," "Thomas" in 1:41,42; 9:7; 11:16), offering background for developments in the narrative and for geographical features[84] and even supplying theological perspectives (e.g., clarifying references from a later standpoint in 2:21-22; 7:39; 11:51-52; 12:16,33; or protecting Jesus' divinity in 6:6,64). Historically, some of these may reflect a situation where a tradition transmitted at first in one context (Palestinian or Jewish) is now being proclaimed in another context (Diaspora or Gentile). As footnotes, they are difficult to read in public; but in the liturgy they offer a marvelous opportunity to reflect on how much pedagogy had to go into the proclamation of the Christian message, since terms known to one group or generation were not known to another group or generation.

I have explained these stylistic features because without attention to them those reading or preaching on John will miss a very important part of the Gospel's communication.

[83] See 1:19 with 1:28; 1:28 with 10:40; 2:11 with 4:54; 9:2-3 with 9:41; 11:4 with 11:40.

[84] For example, 2:9; 3:24; 4:8; 6:71; 9:14,22-23; 11:5,13.

Christ in the Gospels of the Ordinary Sundays

Let me remind readers once more that large portions of John have been treated in previous books in this series (table at the end of this volume). Accordingly I concentrate here on specific passages not discussed in those volumes.

THE PROLOGUE (1:1-18): While Mark is content to begin his Gospel with the heavenly declaration at the baptism that Jesus is God's beloved Son, Matt and Luke start their Good News with an angelic proclamation of Jesus' divine identity at his conception. John reaches back even before creation to identify Jesus as the Word who was God. The church uses this at the third Mass of Christmas and on the last weekday Mass of the Christmas octave in order to bring out the fullest meaning of what that feast reveals. There is no higher understanding of Jesus in the NT than John 1:1, "The Word was God"; and the evangelist will remind us of this by way of inclusion at the end of the Gospel when Thomas confesses Jesus as "My Lord and my God" (20:28).

Serving as a preface to the Gospel, the Prologue is really a hymn that encapsulates the Johannine view of Christ and anticipates what we shall be told in narrative form in the Gospel. A divine being (God's Word [1:1,14], who is also the light [1:5,9] and God's only Son [1:14,18]) comes into the world and becomes flesh. Although rejected by his own, he empowers all who do accept him to become God's children, so that they share in God's fullness—a gift reflecting God's enduring love[85] that outdoes the loving gift of the Law through Moses. One background of this poetic description of the descent of the Word into the world and the eventual return of the Son to the Father's side (1:18) lies in the OT picture of personified Wisdom (especially Sirach 24 and Wisdom 9), who was with God in the

---

[85] The "grace" and "truth" of 1:14 probably reproduce the famous OT pairing of *ḥesed*, that is, God's *kindness* (mercy) in choosing Israel independently of any merit on Israel's part, and *'ĕmet*, God's enduring *fidelity* to the covenant with Israel that embodies this kindness.

Chapter 5. John

beginning at the creation of the world and came to dwell with human beings when the Law was revealed to Moses. In agreement with the tradition that JBap's ministry was related to the beginning of Jesus' ministry, the Prologue is interrupted twice, viz., to mention JBap just before the light comes into the world (1:6-8—JBap is not the light but bears witness to the light) and to record JBap's testimony after the Word becomes flesh (1:15—Jesus existed before JBap).

OPENING DAYS OF THE REVELATION OF JESUS UNDER DIFFERENT TITLES: JBAP AND THE FIRST DISCIPLES (1:19-51). On January 2–5, the days before Epiphany, the Lectionary reads from this section of John, which unfolds the mystery of Jesus in a pattern of separate days (1:29,35,43); part of it is read on the 2d Ordinary Sunday (1:29-34 in A year; 1:35-42 in B). John illustrates a gradual recognition of who Jesus is through testimony by JBap and through confession of their understanding of Jesus by the first disciples. *On the first day* (1:19-28) JBap explains his own role totally in relation to Jesus. JBap becomes briefer and briefer in rejecting titles for himself and voluble only in predicting the coming of one of whom he is unworthy. JBap thus anticipates 3:30: "He must increase while I must decrease." It is noteworthy that a legal atmosphere colors the Johannine narrative from its first page, for JBap is interrogated by "the Jews,"[86] and he testifies and does not deny. As I explained above, this suggests that some of the Johannine tradition was shaped in a forensic context, probably in a synagogue where Christians were put on trial for their beliefs about Jesus. When read in the liturgy it reminds us of our duty to bear witness to Jesus, sometimes in a hostile context, sometimes in an indifferent one. *On the next day* (1:29-34) JBap explains Jesus' role. As befits "one sent by God" (1:6), JBap has special knowledge of Jesus and perceptively recognizes Jesus as the Lamb of God, as one who existed beforehand, and as God's chosen one (or

[86] The evangelist may well be a Jew by birth; yet as pp. 85 and 97 explain, in general he uses this expression with a hostile tone for those of Jewish birth who distrust or reject Jesus and/or his followers.

Christ in the Gospels of the Ordinary Sundays

Son—disputed reading of 1:34). But now JBap must begin his assigned task of revealing Jesus to others who will be Jesus' first disciples.

On the next day (1:35-42) Jesus is followed by Andrew and another disciple of JBap.[87] Andrew hails Jesus as teacher and Messiah and brings his brother Simon to Jesus. Anticipating Simon's role as a disciple (see 6:67-69), Jesus gives him a new identity as "Cephas," using the transliterated Aramaic word for "rock," which equals the Greek name for Peter (cf. Mark 3:16; Matt 16:18). Already this initial scene tells us much about discipleship. Jesus poses an initial question in John 1:38, "What are you looking for?" and follows in 1:39 by "Come and see." Yet it is only when those invited remain with him that they become believers. All that is still true of those who would be disciples today. *On the next day* (1:43-51) Jesus finds Philip, who in turn finds Nathanael; and Jesus is identified as the one described in the Mosaic Law and the Prophets as the Son of God and the King of Israel. (Notice the pattern of discipleship: Those initially called go out to proclaim Jesus to others with a christological perception deepened through that very action.) In Mark (15:39) only after Jesus dies does a human being recognize him as "Son of God," and in Matt (16:16) this is a climactic confession by Peter in the middle of the ministry. In John such confessional titles proclaimed by the disciples at the very beginning, although true, are somewhat elementary; for they do not fully express the divinity of Jesus, the Word who existed before the world began.[88] Thus Jesus promises a vision of "far greater things" and speaks of himself as the Son of Man upon whom the angels ascend and descend. For the other Gospels the sight of the Son of Man accompanied by the

---

[87] Is he the one who by the second part of the Gospel will have become the disciple whom Jesus loved?

[88] The oldest tradition is that the Fourth Gospel was written to improve on the other Gospels. That is too simple, but in terms of christological insight John certainly goes beyond the tradition common to the Synoptics. After all, it claims to stem from a disciple who was closer to Jesus than anyone else.

Chapter 5. John

angels will come only at the end of time; for John that occurs during the ministry because the Son of Man has already come down from heaven. The church is wise liturgically to use John's account of the first days of Jesus shortly after Christmas; it is telling believers that no matter how much they may know about the Christ who has come into the world, if they remain his committed disciples, they have much more to understand.

THE FIRST CANA MIRACLE (2:1-12). The "far greater things" promised by Jesus begin to occur in Cana on the third day after the call of the disciples. The church uses this reading on the 2d Sunday of the Ordinary Time in Year C. In this it is continuing an old liturgical practice of three epiphanies or manifestations of Jesus: On the feast of the Epiphany a star reveals Jesus to the Gentiles; on the next Sunday (1st of the Ordinary Time), which is the feast of the Baptism, a heavenly voice reveals him; now on this following Sunday Jesus reveals himself. In what John calls a sign Jesus replaces the water prescribed for Jewish purifications by wine so good that the headwaiter wonders why the best has been kept until last. This wine represents the revelation and wisdom that Jesus brings from God (Proverbs 9:4-5; Sirach 24:21[20]), fulfilling the OT promises of abundance of wine in the messianic days (Amos 9:13-14; Genesis 49:10-11). And so through it Jesus has manifested his glory, and his disciples believe in him. An intertwined motif involves the mother of Jesus, whose family-style request on behalf of the newly married ("They have no wine") is rebuffed by Jesus on the grounds that his hour had not yet come. Yet the mother's persistence that honors Jesus' terms ("Do whatever he tells you") leads him to grant her original request.[89] She will reappear at the foot of the cross (John 19:25-27), where her incorporation into discipleship will be completed as she becomes the mother of the Beloved Disciple.

---

[89] Similarly in the second Cana sign the royal official's persistence wins his request after a rebuff (John 4:47-50; cf. Mark 7:26-29).

Christ in the Gospels of the Ordinary Sundays

This constitutes most of Part One of the Gospel. Yet now the
liturgical use of John departs from a sequential treatment to a
topical one, and the topics differ in ways from those that the
evangelist planned—see Outline of Part One, above. (This
would be a very appropriate moment for readers to look at a sequential commentary on John, for example, my brief paperback
done for The Liturgical Press: *The Gospel and Epistles of John: A
Concise Commentary*.) Let me discuss three major motifs visible
in the liturgical readings from John's account of the remainder
of the public ministry—with Lent as the principal setting for the
first two.[90]

1. INCREASING CONFLICTS ABOUT JESUS' IDENTITY, LEADING TO
PLOTS TO KILL HIM. These constitute the major part of the weekday Lectionary for the last weeks of Lent, as visible in the table
at the end of the book; they prepare readers for Jesus' death on
Good Friday. In his lifetime Jesus certainly had conflicts with
Pharisees, Jerusalem Jewish authorities, and the parts of the Jerusalem populace that sided with authorities.[91] Nevertheless,
the Gospel represents a situation that goes beyond Jesus' lifetime, and "the Jews" include Jewish authorities but cannot be
confined to them. The expulsion of Johannine Christians from
the synagogue led to a feeling of alienation whereby, even
though they may have been of Jewish parentage, Johannine
Christians no longer were considered or considered themselves
as Jews. For them "the Jews" were those people who opposed
and even persecuted them (16:2) and were the heirs of those
who had opposed Jesus. This usage of "the Jews" is entirely
religious and has nothing to do with racial, economic, or social

---

[90] This public ministry ends in 12:50, but a few passages from the Last Supper (13:1-15,21-33,36-38) are read in Holy Week as the conclusion of Lent.

[91] Attempts to remove all references to "Jews" or to translate them simply as
"the authorities" falsify the historical situation; this was a time when Jews
fought other Jews bitterly over such issues as Temple worship, calendar, and interpretations of the Law, to the point of putting one another to death.

Chapter 5. John

prejudice. It is irresponsible in my judgment to deny that such antagonism existed or to seek to disguise its presence in translations of John;[92] nevertheless, *those who read, interpret, or preach on John in our time must take extreme care to prevent the correct, literal translation from being used against Jewish people in our time.* The historical situation must be explained, and one must insist that the Bible does not always give us examples to be imitated[93] but at times examples to be learned from painfully.

2. DRAMATIC STORIES OF FAITH RESPONSES. For many centuries, dating back to the ancient Jerusalem liturgy, the church has singled out stories from John to be read with special solemnity during Lent. In our era three of them—the most sacred *narratives* in the Gospel accounts of Jesus' public ministry—appear on the 3d, 4th, and 5th Sundays of Lent in the A Year (with special provisions made for the B and C years, so that there may never be a Lent in which they are not proclaimed). They are the Samaritan woman at the well (John 4), the healing of the man born blind (John 9), and the raising of Lazarus (John 11). During the Lenten season from the earliest days people were being prepared for baptism, and John's stories fitted beautifully into the process of Christian initiation. In time, the three narratives were read at specific stages in the Lenten preparation of catechumens for baptism on Holy Saturday.[94]

The woman at the well: Coming to faith and living water. This first story (John 4:1-42) illustrates how difficult it is to come to Jesus in faith because of the various obstacles that stand in the way. If I were freely composing a story of conversion, I might

[92] The Johannine Jesus at times speaks as a non-Jew (or, at least, not as one of *those* "Jews"): "written in your Law" (10:34); "in their Law" (15:25); "as I said to the Jews" (13:33).

[93] Compare the many OT examples of Israel's rejoicing at the slaughter of other peoples who occupied Palestine.

[94] The material pertaining to these three stories is taken from a *Catholic Update,* reused as Chapter Four in my *Reading the Gospels with the Church* (Cincinnati, St. Anthony Messenger Press, 1996). That press has graciously allowed me to draw on it here.

Christ in the Gospels of the Ordinary Sundays

imagine a central character eager to receive God. John is more realistic: Many people have a chip on their shoulder in regard to God because they feel beaten down by the inequalities in life. The woman smarts from the Jewish dislike for Samaritans, especially for Samaritan women. And that is her first obstacle to dealing with Jesus. "How can you, a Jew," she comments sarcastically, "ask me, a Samaritan woman, for a drink?" Jesus does not answer her objection; he is not going to change instantly a whole world of injustice. Yet he can offer something that will enable the woman to put injustice in perspective, namely, living water. He means water that gives life; she misunderstands it as flowing, bubbling water, contemptuously asking him if he thinks he is greater than Jacob, who provided a well. (Is not "No thanks—I already have all I need" our first reaction when someone tries to interest us in something new religiously?)

Ironically, as John expects the reader to recognize, Jesus is greater than Jacob; but again Jesus refuses to be sidetracked from his main goal, and so he explains that he is speaking of the water that springs up to eternal life, a water that will permanently end thirst. With masterful touch John shows her attracted on a level of the convenience of not having to come to the well every day for water. (People are not so different today when they are attracted to the message of those media evangelists who promote a religion that makes life more comfortable.) To move the woman to a higher level, Jesus shifts the focus to her husband. Her reply is a half-truth, but Jesus shows that he is aware of her five husbands and of her live-in who is not her husband. Today also, a far-from-perfect past is not an uncommon obstacle to conversion. To be brought to faith people must acknowledge where they stand, but they can take hope from the fact that Jesus persists even though he knows the woman's state. He does not say to the woman, "Come back after you straighten out your life," for the grace that he offers is meant to help her to change.

Confronted with Jesus' surprising knowledge of her situation, the woman seeks to take advantage of the fact that he is obviously a religious figure. Her question about whether to worship in the Jerusalem Temple or on Mount Gerizim is a typical ploy designed to distract. When is the last time she worried about such theological differences? Even today when we encounter someone who probes our lives, we are often adept at bringing up as a distraction some old religious chestnut so as to avoid making a decision. Once more Jesus refuses to be sidetracked. Although salvation is from the Jews, a time is coming and is now here when such a cultic issue is irrelevant: Cult at both sites will be replaced by worship in Spirit and truth. Nimbly the woman tries one more ploy by shifting any decision to the distant future when the Messiah comes, but Jesus will not let her escape. His "I am he" confronts her with a current demand for faith.

What follows, enacted dramatically on two stages, reveals even more about faith. In center stage we observe that the disciples who have now been with Jesus for some time understand his heavenly symbolism no better than the woman who encountered him for the first time. When he speaks of the food that he already has to eat, they wonder if someone has brought him a sandwich! Jesus has to explain: "My food is to do the will of the One who sent me . . ." (John 4:34). On side stage, we find that the woman is still not fully convinced, since she poses to the villagers the question "Could this be the Messiah?" The villagers come and encounter Jesus for themselves, so that their faith is not simply dependent on her account but on personal contact. We are left to surmise that by being instrumental in bringing others to believe the woman's own faith came to completion. And at last she drank of the water of life.

The man born blind: Faith grows amidst trials. If the story of the Samaritan woman has illustrated an initial coming to faith, this next carefully crafted narrative (9:1-41) shows that often first enlightenment does not result in adequate faith. Sometimes faith comes only through difficult testing and even suffering. St. Augustine recognized that this man born blind stands for the human race. And the initial dialogue where Jesus proclaims, "I

Christ in the Gospels of the Ordinary Sundays

am the light of the world" alerts us to the fact that more than physical sight is involved. The basic story of the man's healing is simple. Jesus approaches the blind man, anoints his eyes with mud mixed with saliva, and tells him to wash in the Pool of Siloam. The man does so and comes back seeing.

Beyond this, however, the early Christian community who first heard John's account probably picked out elements of their own conversion and baptism in the blind man's story. They might recognize something familiar, for example, in the blind man's coming to see the light by being "anointed." Anointing became a part of baptism very early; and "enlightenment" was a term for baptismal conversion, as we see in Hebrews 6:4; 10:32 and in the 2d-century writer Justin. John hints further that the water has a special link with Christ, since he tells us that "Siloam," the name of the pool, means "the one sent," a frequent description of Jesus. No wonder that in early catacomb art the healing of the blind man was a symbol of baptism!

Besides recognizing a baptismal theme in this story, readers of John would also be taught that a series of testings may be necessary before sight really comes. Only gradually and through suffering does the man born blind come to full faith and enlightenment. There are at least four steps in his progress, each involving an encounter: (1) At first, when queried by the onlookers, the man born blind knows only that "the man they call Jesus" healed him (9:11). (2) Then, brought before the Pharisees and pressed with theological questions, he advances to the conclusion that Jesus is "a prophet" (9:17). (3) Next, after being threatened with expulsion from the synagogue, he recognizes that Jesus is a man "from God" (9:33). (4) Finally, having been expelled, he encounters Jesus himself, who has sought him out and now asks point-blank, "Do you believe in the Son of Man?" It is then at last that the man says, "I do believe" (9:38: perhaps the baptismal confession required in the Johannine church).

How many of us who have a traditional faith stemming from our baptism come to believe in our hearts only when difficult decisions test our faith in God and Christ? It is then we

Chapter 5. John

101

understand what it means to say, "I do believe." Yet within John's story it is not only from the man born blind that we learn about faith. His being healed produces a division (Greek *krisis*, whence English "crisis") among those who interrogate him. In the Johannine view an encounter with Jesus or his work forces people to decide and align themselves on one side or the other. Particularly interesting is the division caused among the Pharisees (9:13-17). John presents favorably those Pharisees who decide that Jesus cannot be sinful because he does such signs (healings), but we should also seek to understand the other Pharisees who decide that Jesus is not from God because he does not keep the Sabbath. Their thinking probably went along these lines: God commanded that the Sabbath be kept holy; our ancestors decided that kneading clay was menial work that violated the Sabbath; Jesus kneaded clay on the Sabbath, and so he violated God's commandment. Might not faithful Christians today judge along similar lines if someone violated what they had been taught as a traditional interpretation of God's will? (And might they not be offended if their decisions were greeted with the sarcasm with which the man born blind reacted to the Jewish authorities' decision about Jesus?) The difficulty with such reasoning is the failure to recognize that all human interpretations of God's will are historically conditioned—those we regard as definitive tradition are *true*, but *in regard to the issues that were in mind when they were formulated*. Hebrew slaves in Egypt had to work with clay to make bricks for the pharaoh, and so kneading clay would justly be classified as servile work forbidden on the Sabbath. But those who made that classification scarcely thought of kneading a scrap of clay to open a blind man's eyes. Jesus is the type of figure who raises new religious issues and inevitably causes offense to those who attempt to solve those issues quickly on the basis of previous situations. Recognition of that should facilitate important insights. It was not necessarily out of malice that many genuinely religious people of Jesus' time (who were Jews because of where they lived) rejected him. If Jesus came back today, he would be

Christ in the Gospels of the Ordinary Sundays

equally offensive to religious people of our time, including Christians. We should be careful about religious judgments that apply, without nuance, past decisions to *new* situations.

Finally, we can learn about faith from the parents of the blind man. John contrasts the man born blind, who step-by-step was brought to sight physically and spiritually, with the opposing religious authorities, who could see physically but gradually became blind spiritually (9:40-41). Yet the evangelist is also interested in those who refuse to commit themselves one way or the other. The parents know the truth about their son, but they refuse to say anything about what Jesus has done for him lest they be thrown out of the synagogue. Today there are those who decide for Jesus at a great cost to themselves and those who for various reasons do not believe in him. Perhaps an even larger group would be those who have been baptized and nominally accept Jesus but are not willing to confess him if it costs anything. In John's view that is as serious as to deny him.

The raising of Lazarus: Faith tested by death. As we come to the final narrative (John 11:1-44), we should take note of the different staging techniques in the three stories. The Samaritan woman remained close to Jesus for much of the drama at the well and entered into a fairly long dialogue with him. The man born blind said nothing to Jesus at the beginning, was not in contact with him through most of the scene, and exchanged words with Jesus only at the end in a moment of piercing light when he confessed Jesus. Lazarus never says a word to Jesus (or anyone else) and appears only in the last verses. In each story we are dealing with a different stage of faith. The Samaritan woman illustrated an initial coming to faith; the man born blind illustrated an incipient faith that acquired depth only after testing; the Lazarus story illustrates *the deepening of faith that comes from facing death.* John tells the Lazarus story in such a way that we are led to a more profound understanding of death even as the disciples and Martha and Mary had to intensify their understanding. Like his sisters, Martha and Mary, Lazarus was loved

Chapter 5. John

by Jesus; and so when he dies, the disciples are troubled by Jesus' seeming indifference. They misunderstand when he speaks of Lazarus' sleep. As with blindness in John 9 (of which we are reminded in 11:37), life and death are used to teach about earthly and heavenly realities.

Martha, who is the chief dialogue partner in the drama, already believes that Jesus is the Messiah, the Son of God, and that her brother, Lazarus, will participate in the resurrection on the last day. Yet hers is an incomplete faith, for she wishes that her brother had never died and hesitates when Jesus orders Lazarus' tomb opened. Jesus can and does bring Lazarus back to earthly life, but that is not his purpose in having come to this world from above. (A man brought back from the grave is not necessarily better off or closer to God than those who have not yet died.) Jesus comes *to give life that cannot be touched by death,* so that those who believe in him will never die (11:26). True faith has to include a belief in Jesus as the source of unending life. Such immortality, however, cannot come in Jesus' public ministry; it awaits Jesus' own resurrection. Consequently, we encounter more unexplained symbolism in the Lazarus narrative than was present in the stories of the Samaritan woman and the man born blind. We are never told, for instance, that Martha and Mary came to understand fully Jesus' words, "I am the life." In another instance we hear that Jesus shuddered, seemingly with anger, when he saw Mary and her Jewish friends weeping. But the evangelist does not clarify why Jesus reacts in this way at what seems like well-intentioned grief (11:33,38). Nor does John supply an interpretation of why Lazarus emerges from the tomb tied hand and foot with burial bands and his face wrapped in a cloth (11:44). Only when we read the account of Jesus' tomb in 20:6-7 does that symbolism become clear. Jesus rises to eternal life, never to die again; therefore he leaves behind in the tomb his burial wrappings and the piece that covered his head, for which he has no need. Lazarus was brought back to life enveloped in burial clothes because he was going to die again.

Christ in the Gospels of the Ordinary Sundays

Thus, although the raising of Lazarus is a tremendous miracle bringing to culmination Jesus' ministry, it is still a sign. The life to which Lazarus is raised is natural life; it is meant to symbolize eternal life, the kind of life that only God possesses and that Jesus as God's Son makes possible. How does this fit into Lenten reflections on faith? Even after the struggles of initial faith (the Samaritan woman) and a faith made mature through testing (the man born blind), facing death often constitutes a unique challenge to belief. Whether the death of a loved one or one's own death, it is the moment where one realizes that all depends on God. No human support goes with one to the grave; credit cards, health insurance, retirement programs, and human companionship stop at the tomb. One enters alone. If there is no God, there is nothing; if Christ has not conquered death, there is no future. The brutality of that realization causes trembling even among those who have spent their lives professing Christ, and it is not unusual for people to confess that doubts have come into their minds as they face death. Paul cries out that death is the last enemy to be overcome (1 Corinthians 15:26), an insight that John captures by placing the Lazarus story at the end of Jesus' public ministry. From it we learn that no matter how fervently catechumens or already baptized Christians make or renew a baptismal profession in Lent, they may still face a last moment when their faith will be tested. For so many of us it will be precisely at that moment, when we are confronted with the visible reality of the grave, that we need to hear and embrace the bold message that Jesus proclaims in John's Gospel: "I am the life." Despite all human appearances, "Everyone who believes in me shall never die at all." We begin Lent with the reminder that we will return to dust. We end at Easter with the proclamation of new life.

3. BAPTISMAL AND EUCHARISTIC MOTIFS. In a previous work in this series, *A Once and Coming Spirit at Pentecost*, I discussed the Nicodemus dialogue in John 3:1-21 and the multiplication of the loaves/Bread of Life discourse in John 6:1-69 as they are used in the weekday readings of the postEaster weeks. The baptismal

gift of life and the eucharistic nourishment of that life flow from the resurrection, whence the placement.

Passages from the rest of the Gospel of John (the Book of Glory, plus the Epilogue [13:1–21:25]) are read in the liturgy of Good Friday and of the Eastertime. They have already been discussed in three books of this liturgical series (see table at the end of this book).

Christ in the Gospels of the Ordinary Sundays

SIMPLIFIED TABLE OF USE OF THE GOSPELS IN THE SUNDAY AND SEASONAL MASS LECTIONARY

Liturgical Season	Matthew (chapters)	Mark (chapters)	Luke (chapters)	John (chapters)	Where Treated in R. E. Brown's Liturgical Press Series
LAST WEEK OF ADVENT	1		1		COMING CHRIST IN ADVENT
Christmas and Octave (Epiphany; Presentation)	2		2	3d Xmas Mass: (and Dec. 31) Prologue: 1:1-18	ADULT CHRIST AT CHRISTMAS (for Matt and Luke); THIS BOOK for John
Baptism (=1st Ordinary Sunday)	3:13-17	1:7-11	3:15-16, 21-22		THIS BOOK
2d Ordinary Sunday				1:29-42; 2:1-12†	THIS BOOK
Ordinary Sundays before Lent (beginning with 3d Sunday)††	YEAR A first part of 4-25 (beginning with 4:12)	YEAR B first part of 1-13 (beginning with 1:14)	YEAR C first part of 4-21 (beginning with 4:14)		THIS BOOK
Last Weeks of Lent (Weekdays and Sundays)†††				2:13-12:50 (plus parts of 13)	THIS BOOK
Passion (Palm) Sunday Good Friday	26-27	14-15	22-23	18-19	CRUCIFIED CHRIST IN HOLY WEEK
Easter Sunday and Octave	28	16	24	20-21	RISEN CHRIST IN EASTERTIME
2d-7th Weeks of Easter Time (Weekdays and Sundays)				3; 6; and 10; Last Discourse: 13:31-17:26	ONCE AND COMING SPIRIT AT PENTECOST
Ordinary Sundays after Pentecost	later parts of 4-25	later parts of 1-13 (interrupted for five Sundays by John 6)	later parts of 4-21	(see under Mark)	THIS BOOK

†John 1:19-51 is read on January 2-5, a fluctuating period depending on the date of the 1st Ordinary Sunday, on which Epiphany is celebrated.
††See explanation of this beginning on pp. 12-14 above.
†††John is read in Lent on the 3d and 4th Sundays (A, B years) and 5th (A, B, C). John is read on Lenten weekdays from Monday of the 4th week to Tuesday of Holy Week (from 4:43 to 13:38).

Index of Discussion of Gospel Readings Used on Ordinary Sundays

Index of Discussion

Index of Discussion of Readings from John

Works of Raymond E. Brown published by The Liturgical Press

A Coming Christ in Advent (Matthew 1 and Luke 1)
An Adult Christ at Christmas (Matthew 2 and Luke 2)
A Crucified Christ in Holy Week (Passion Narratives)
A Risen Christ in Eastertime (Resurrection Narratives)
A Once-and-Coming Spirit at Pentecost (Acts and John)
Christ in the Gospels of the Ordinary Sundays

The Gospels and Epistles of John: A Concise Commentary
Recent Discoveries and the Biblical World (A Michael Glazier Book)
The New Jerome Bible Handbook, edited with J. A. Fitzmyer and
    R. E. Murphy